WASHINGTON'S EYES

THE CONTINENTAL
LIGHT DRAGOONS

By Burt Garfield Loescher

THE OLD ARMY PRESS

Library of Congress Catalog Card No. LC 76-9410

ISBN 0-88342-051-1

Published jointly by

THE OLD ARMY PRESS
1513 Welch
Fort Collins, Colo. 80521

The Military Shop
LAKEWOOD SHOPPING CENTER
5234 PEPPERWOOD AVE.
LAKEWOOD, CA 90712

CONTENTS

LIST OF ILLUSTRATIONS

BOOKS BY THE AUTHOR:
The History of Rogers Rangers 1755-1758
Genesis-Rogers Rangers-The First Green Berets 1758-1783
Officers & Non-Commissioned Officers of Rogers Rangers 1755-1761
Washington's Eyes-The Continental Light Dragoons

BOOKS IN PREPARATION

Abenaki Aphrodite-Rogers' St. Francis Raid-Fact, Legend, & Lost Treasure
Rogers Ranger Diary of Lieutenant George Campbell
edited with Notes by Burt G. Loescher
Rogers Rangers-The Explorers & Discoverers
Officers & Men of Rogers Rangers
Ranger Goodwin's Rum-A Novel of Collected Tales

ART (Satire & Instruction)
How to be a Famous Painter Without Being Insane

NOVEL
Thompson Seedless

Illustrations: Notes & Credits

The illustrative scences depicting each of the four Continental Light Dragoon Regiments (on Title page and Chapter heading pages) are by the very gifted Artist and Model Miniature Designer Clyde A. Risley. Risley has that unique flair for *telling a story* in his paintings and illustrations. An ability of technique that elevates his work above the customary *uniform plate*. One is assured of the most minute accuracy in all of his military creations. So much so, that his historical drawings are *the Design* for the creation of the superbly designed Model Miniatures by the IMRIE/RISLEY MINIATURES, Incorporated (425-A Oak St., Copiague, N.Y. 11726).

54MM scale Models of the four Contintenal Light Dragoon Regiments may be obtained with the illustrations reproduced in this book on 4x5½ cards with most of the uniform data reproduced in this book for each regiment on reverse side for the coloring guide of their Model Miniatures of the Dragoons.

The Battle of Cowpens-Conflict between Cols. Washington and Tarleton (page 88) from the original picture by Chappel in the possession (1858) of the publishers: Johnson Fry & Company, N.Y. Alonzo Chappel was the noted Romanticist painter of the American historical scene. Popular in his era, his paintings are now much sought after by the burgeoning crop of Americanists.

Pewter Uniform Button of The 3rd Continental Light Dragoons (page 72) facsimile. Discovered in excavation "diggings" at the Old Tappan Massacre site.

American Cavalry (of Lee's Legion) under the command of Henry "Light Horse Harry" Lee at Guilford (page 17) is a possible depiction of Lee's troop as they appeared in 1776-1778 as a troop of the First Continental Light Dragoons as this troop formed the nucleous of "Lee's Legion" in the spring of 1778 and removed from Bland's Horse.

TO MY WIFE HELENE
and to that new breed of 'Patriots'
Steve, Bridget, Mark, Dave & Joe
This Book is
Affectionately dedicated

INTRODUCTION

General Washington's regular cavalry, the four Continental Light Dragoon regiments authorized by the Continental Congress were the eyes of his army.

The story of their impact in our struggle for freedom has never been fully told. The story of each unit was a distinctive one, fascinating in their exploits as well as their pathos of sheer tragedy.

Though the terrain of conflict generally lacked the openness of the far west where cavalry tactics in the later plains Indian wars were the principal mode of attack, still, the sites of many decisive Revolutionary war battles were ideal for cavalry manouvering.

Three factors stymied the concerted employment of the four Dragoon regiments as a tactical brigade of cavalry, particularly in the decisive Pennsylvania-New Jersey campaigns of 1777-1778: They were the distrust of the constant devaluing Continental dollar so that the purchase of horses and equipment was always extremely difficult. The scarcity of fodder for the constant moving cavalry was ever present. Lastly, there was the lack of early dynamic leadership. Washington had it in Count Casimir Pulaski, but Pulaski's lack of ability to integrate his Polish officers with the American Dragoon officers already in the field compromised his leadership. Principally because of the language barrier and the utterly rude overbearing manner of his Polish staff, who considered themselves far superior to the Americans.

The brilliant American cavalry leadership came later, particularly under Lieutenant Colonel William Washington and Major Benjamin Tallmadge. William Washington became the Murat of the American Dragoons when, after seeing the almost decimitation of his regiment, not once but twice, by the surprise attack of the hated British partisan Tarleton, revived his remnants to later strike a crushing, brilliantly manouvered charge against Tarleton at Cowpens. Commanding the First and Third Dragoons in Greene's literal *commando army*, William Washington, until his capture, was most instrumental in holding the south until Yorktown.

The other field officers, for the most part, were denied the opportunity of similar battle leadership. Their energy draining tasks were that of constant re-supply and recruitment for their regiments. The Colonels, Stephen Moylan, Elisha Sheldon, and Walton White were heroic in their never ending efforts to maintain their regiments in the field. Colonel Sheldon even risking gaol for his efforts.

It invariably fell upon the Captains and Lieutenants with troop (or skeleton troop) strength detachments to make telling strikes against the British and Loyalist forces from Connecticut to far away Georgia.

One other field officer, Major Benjamin Tallmadge of the Second Dragoons, equalled William Washington in the risking of life. Tallmadge's mode of operindi was more varied for he not only executed extremely successful whaleboat strikes to Long Island, he also, under a code name headed General Washington's secret service link in Connecticut from New York City. His tale of his espionage service is an incredible one. He was truly Washington's eyes, as were the other Dragoons from the four regiments in his secret service.

The saga of Washington's Dragoon regiments is a fascinating one. Each unit had their own uniquely compelling story. . . . .

Burt Garfield Loescher
San Mateo, California

Part One
BLAND'S VIRGINIA HORSE

THE FIRST CONTINENTAL LIGHT DRAGOONS

These First Dragoons of Washington's Continental Light Dragoon regiments may have been favoured by Washington as they both shared Virginia for their origin. If this was not enough for partisanship, the regiments' fame would have placed them first in their Commander-in-Chief's eyes, for their reknown as well as their numerical *first*.

The saga of the First Continental Light Dragoons begins in June of 1776, when Governor Patrick Henry, that Virginia firebrand of the American Revolution, authorized the formation of a volunteer cavalry battalion, of six troops, for the defense of that commonwealth. The unit was commanded and formed by Major-Commandant Theodorick Bland, who had served conspicuously in the expulsion of Lord Dunmore, the former royal governor. The other officers were respected patriots and land owners. Of particular note, was the captain of the fifth troop, Bland's cousin, twenty-year-old Henry Lee, soon to become famous as "Light Horse Harry".

Congress and even Washington had considered cavalry an expensive and unprofitable arm. Washington had even sent home the one available volunteer regiment, the Connecticut Light Dragoons, in somewhat cavalier fashion that July and missed them soon thereafter when the British easily enveloped his position on Long Island. It should be noted that at the beginning, Washington expected more from the cavalry service. While he would condone the leveling-equality spirit between officers and men in his infantry, still, any such familiarity in the horse service, which he considered an elite gentleman officered service with a minimum of familiarity with the rank and file. The observance of a Captain of the Connecticut Horse shaving one of his men on the parade ground before his headquarters shocked him. This unpardonable act and lack of decorum instigated his release of the Connecticut Militia Dragoons. Now, aware of this new battalion, composed of his native Virginians, and therefore presumably of excellent riders and well mounted, Washington asked Patrick Henry for its transfer to his army. However, it was not until after considerable argument among the enlisted men and a great deal of persuasion by their officers and Governor Henry, that the regiment finally consented to serve outside of its native state.

Bland's Virginia Horse, as it was then called, was not fully equipped, but Washington was urgent, and December 1776 saw it on the march to join him.

Bland's return at this time stated that two uniforms were worn at this time: brown faced with green, and blue faced with red. Gradually, as the cloth became available, the regiment were all

4

Colonel Theodorick Bland
First Continental Light Dragoons

The court House at Baltimore, Maryland has hanging
the following post-Revolutionary War oil portrait.
(Courtesy of the Frick Art Reference Library.)
A miniature of Bland was painted in 1777 by Charles
Willson Peale but is unlocated, which is unfortunate as
it undoubtedly would have shown him in his 1st
Dragoon uniform.

Captain "Light Horse Harry Lee"
From the painting by Charles Willson Peale
Independence Hall Historical Park Collection

clothed in the latter color.

Bland's Horse reported to Washington at Morristown where he had encamped after his sudden Trenton-Princeton campaign, to maintain pressure on the British forces remaining in northern New Jersey. Here, after a bleak, hungry, and barefoot winter, the regiment was mustered into the regular Continental service on 31 March 1777, under the authority granted Washington by Congress to raise "3,000 light horse." Major-Commandant Bland was promoted to Colonel, all officers received commissions from Congress, and the battalion was redesignated the First Continental Light Dragoons. Originally it was stipulated that each dragoon would enlist for three years or the duration of the war, and receive twenty dollars and the promise of a hundred acres of land upon discharge. Because of this bounty, there seemed to have been little reluctance to change from State to Continental service. However, a shortage of recruits and replacements soon inaugurated shorter enlistment periods from one year to as low as six months in some instances.

CAMPAIGN OF 1777

The First Continental Light Dragoons were stationed near Bound Brook, about a mile in advance of the intrenched position occupied by the American army along the first range of the Watchung Mountains around Middlebrook. Small detachments scouted across the Raritan River toward the British forces in New Brunswick, ten miles away.

During the middle of May, Captain Henry Lee and his troop were temporarily attached to General Lincoln's brigade in the vicinity of Bound Brook. Here it was so useful that Lincoln detained it, even after Bland had ordered Lee to Chatham to cover the extreme northern flank of the American line. He released the troop only when Howe sailed from New York on 23 July on the confused and confusing voyage which finally brought him to Head of Elk in Chesapeake Bay. Prior to this date the First dragoons were in the preliminary manouvres at Woodbridge and Short Hills, New Jersey in late June.

7

The First Dragoons then moved southward with Washington's army to defend Philadelphia. As the army paraded through that city, a troop of the Dragoons led its march.

At Wilmington the following day, Washington began his reconnaissance of the newly-landed British forces. Among the patrols sent out by the four Continental Light Dragoon regiments was Captain Lee and troop of forty-three men. In the Regiment's first recorded action in August 28, 1776, Lee cut off one of the British foraging and scouting parties, capturing twenty-four prisoners whom he immediately brought to Washington, arriving at ten o'clock that night. Washington thereafter frequently used that aggressive young cavalryman for special assignments.

During the Battle of Brandywine, the Regiment, weakened by detachments to various brigade and division commanders for escort and courier duty, covered Painter's Ford on the right of the American army. American reconnaissance was poorly organized, but it was Colonel Bland himself who discovered the British envelopment of the American right flank in time to enable the Americans to change front to meet it and convert a probable rout into a stubborn withdrawal.

During the interval between this battle and Howe's entry into Philadelphia, Captain Lee and four of his Dragoons were dispatched to burn some flour mills before they fell into enemy hands. Washington's aide, Lieutenant Colonel Alexander Hamilton, joined them as a diversion from staff duties. Crossing the Schuylkill, they accomplished their mission, but were caught by elements of the British 16th and 17th Light Dragoons while recrossing the river. Hamilton became separated from Lee during the skirmish. However, all managed to escape.

Before the Battle of Germantown, on 4 October, the First Continental Light Dragoons were honored by Washington's request that Captain Lee's troop be detailed as his bodyguard during the coming action. Bland and the remainder of his regiment served with portions of the three other Dragoon regiments under the newly appointed "Commander of the Horse", Brigadier General Count Casimir Pulaski. Attempting to cover the final American withdrawal, they were ridden over by British cavalry and stampeded back through the American infantry in the thick fog, further compounding the confusion. Captain Lee and his troop remained near the scene of the battle, maintaining contact with the British forces and gathering estimates of British losses.

The rest of the campaign saw detachments of the Regiment reconnoitering along the New Jersey bank of the Delaware, harassing enemy foraging parties and foraging for the American army. As usual, Lee did well. For three weeks in December, his troop operated with Morgan's riflemen in a series of raids.

CAMPAIGN OF 1778

Because of the scarcity of forage, Washington decided to billet the Dragoon regiments near Trenton, New Jersey, for the winter. There they were scattered across the countryside, seldom in units larger than a single troop, wherever they could obtain shelter and food for themselves and their horses.

Throughout the winter, the First dragoons were distinguished by the exploits of Lee and his troop from their quarters at Scott's Farm, six miles from the summit of Mount Joy in Pennsylvania. Lee's post being the most advanced, he had constant opportunities to harass British foraging detachments, and "Light Horse Harry" and his men were soon receiving praise in the American press.

A troop of Dragoons in Bland's Regiment, seldom having more than 25 men and horses fit for dty, has since the first of August last, taken 124 British and Hessian privates, besides 4 commissioned officers, with the loss of only one horse. This gallant corps is under the command of Captain Lee, Lieutenant Lindsay and Cornet Peyton, whose merits and services it is hoped will not be passed unnoticed or unrewarded. (N.J. Gazette, 14 January 1778)

Finally, Lee became such a nuisance that Simcoe, an outstanding British partisan officer, was ordered out from Philadelphia with his own Loyalist Queen's Rangers and a part of the British 17th Light Dragoon to suppress him. Simcoe's command left Philadelphia on the night of 19 January, two hundred strong. By taking a round-about twenty-five mile route which by-passed Lee's sentries, the

9

British arrived at Scott's Farm as dawn was breaking over the snow-clad slopes. Fortunately, one of Lee's men saw them in time, and the Farmhouse doors were immediately barred. Though Lee had only two officers, a quartermaster sergeant, and four dragoons with him, the rest of his troop being absent on a foraging expedition, he posted them so as to guard all entrances and repulsed two attacks killing or wounding eight British. When the rebuffed attackers tried at least to carry off Lee's horses from the barn, Lee called for a volley, shouting "Fire away, men. Here comes our infantry; we'll have them all . . ." then led a counterattack. Completely bluffed, the British spurred away, without looking back to check the truth of Lee's assertion. The only American casualty was Lieutenant Lindsay, shot in the hand.

In February, Lee was ordered to Delaware to collect forage and supplies, including droves of cattle, for the starving troops at Valley Forge. His troop had become very popular and much in demand for missions requiring enterprise and skill.

The First Dragoons saw their second action of the year in March, when Washington directed Pulaski to send a troop of cavalry to reinforce Wayne on a foraging expedition within the British lines. Selecting a troop of the First Dragoons, Pulaski took command of it in person, joining Wayne at Haddonfield, near Camden, New Jersey. That night, a British force, reported as 3,000 men, slipped across the Delaware and attacked the Americans, but was repulsed. Pulaski charged repeatedly at the head of his dragoons with considerable effect, especially when the enemy was preparing to recross the river. His bravery and intrepidity, as well as that of his First Dragoons, were heartily commended by Wayne in his official report.

On 7 April 1778, the Regiment lost "Light Horse Harry" and his troop. Congress had rewarded him by designating them as the nucleus of a new picked corps, "Lee's Legion". Lee himself was promoted to major.

The First Dragoons, like the other mounted regiments, played an undecisive role throughout the spring of 1778. Split up into many tiny detachments to "watch the movements of the British," they were not involved to their full potential during the Battle of Monmouth. Although they harassed the retreating British all the

Count Casimir Pulaski
General of Cavalry

way to Sandy Hook, they were still able to embark and sail to safety in New York City.

This campaign at an end, the First Dragoons were stationed at their old post at Bound Brook to observe the British forces in New York and intercept the attempts of New Jersey loyalists to smuggle food into that city. Later, the Regiment was quartered for the winter at Winchester, Virginia. Most of the men's enlistments were up, and it was hoped that leave to spend the winter with their families would encourage them to reenlist.

CAMPAIGN OF 1779

This inducement had an effect just the opposite of the one intended. Home looked too good. In March, the First Dragoons mustered only eighty men fit for duty. At this time the Regiment received orders assigning it to General Lincoln's army in South Carolina, but it was July before it was equipped and ready to march. That same month, Colonel Bland was placed in charge of the Saratoga "Convention Prisoners," Lieutenant Colonel Benjamin Temple taking over the command in his place.

Joining Lincoln in time for his bumbled attack on Savannah, Georgia, the Regiment took part in the assault of 9 October. Comprising part of the combined cavalry of the American army under Pulaski they charged vigorously in the center of the French-American line, attempting to penetrate between two redoubts and take the British fortifications from the rear. However, the British fire was too deadly effective. The attack failed completely and the Allies withdrew.

Thereafter, the First Continental Light Dragoons and the Virginia infantry were detached to Augusta, Georgia, where they remained until the British approached Charleston, South Carolina, in February 1780.

CAMPAIGN OF 1780

Ordered to the defense of Charleston, the First Dragoons, now commanded by Major John Jameson, arrived in early February. They were stationed with the rest of the American cavalry (altogether 379 officers and men, including the Third Continental Light Dragoons) about twenty-four miles from Charleston at Bacon's Bridge across the Ashely River. Under General Moultrie, they were instrumental in removing the horses, cattle, wagons, boats, and other articles that would be of use to the British. This involved a number of brisk skirmishes. After Clinton began his investment of Charleston, the combined American cavalry fell back to Monck's Corner to General Huger's command. Here, now numbering about 500. The portion of First and Third Dragoons were temporarily led by Lieutenant Colonel William Washington, the senior field officer of the two regiments. They were to guard the fords of the Cooper River and hold open a possible line of retreat for Lincoln's forces in Charleston.

Initially successful against Banastre Tarleton's ill-mounted British Legion cavalry, the First and Third Dragoons were surprised at three o'clock of the morning of 14 April and completely routed. Part of the command escaped into the swamps and rallied north of the Santee River. There Lieutenant Colonel Anthony W. White joined them and assumed command as the senior Dragoon officer present (he had been transferred from the Fourth Continental Light Dragoons to the First).

Collecting the scattered dragoons, White remounted them on the excellent horses available in the neighborhood, and then proceeded to attack the enemy's foraging parties on the south side of the Santee. After capturing one large party, he was surprised by Tarleton at Lenud's Ferry while awaiting boats and thoroughly defeated as at Monck's Corner. While part of his command again escaped into the nearby swamps and swam the Santee, its strength was so reduced that it had to withdraw to recruit. Shortly thereafter, Charleston capitulated, and these remaining First and Third American Dragoons withdrew into North Carolina.

Here the few remaining troopers of the First Dragoons were placed under the command of Captain John Watts and served with

Lieutenant Colonel Anthony Walton White
Commanding First Continental Light Dragoons,
1779-1780

An excellent engraving from the pastel portrait by
James Sharples, a well known portraitist who arrived in
America in 1796, traveling throughout the new Republic painting portraits. White's high collar, the Cincin-
nati medal, and full-crested helmet establish the painting as done in the 1790's, probably in 1799 when White
was commissioned Brigadier General of the emergency
army.

William Washington's Third Continental Light Dragoon regiment. With this organization they shared in the incredible hardships and glories of Greene's southern campaigns in the battles of Cowpens (where they were the decisive factor in completely routing Tarleton) Guilford, Hobkirk's Hill and Eutaw Springs, where Watts was wounded.

Lieutenant Colonel White and the other officers of the First Dragoons returned to Virginia, where Steuben was desperately trying to raise reinforcements for Greene's southern army. White hoped to recreate the First Dragoons to regimental strength, but it was heartbreakingly slow going. There were so many obstacles in the way. The Virginia Assembly, for example, had passed a law limiting the price of horses for the cavalry at $150,000 Continental (or $150 hard money) — a sum that would not buy even the worst sort of crowbait.

CAMPAIGN OF 1781

Clothing and weapons were equally expensive, but White furnished money from his own pocket to enable his Regiment to take the field. By May, when Lafayette arrived to oppose Cornwallis, White had recruited 200 men, but it was the end of July before he had enough horses to mount them all — and he still had not procured enough arms and uniforms to put them into the field. Eventually, the principal uniform of the First Continental Light Dragoons to the close of the war was: —

HELMET—Brass, without visor, surmounted by a long white horsehair crest with black bearskin around the base (not all the men were fortunate enough to obtain this type).
HAIR—Natural color, or powdered white for dress occasions.
NECK STOCK—Black.
COAT—Dark blue faced with red on the collar, lapels, cuffs and coat tail turnbacks. Silver buttons of pewter. As customary for the era, the Trumpeteer may have been dressed in reverse facings, viz., a red coat with dark blue collar, lapels, cuffs and coat turnbacks. The southern company under Captain Watts wore a white fringed hunting shirt while serving in William

Washington's command in Greene's army.

VEST—Red.

BREECHES—Buff (usually, leather or cloth.

BOOTS—Black leather with silver colored spurs.

SABER AND BELT—Silver hilt with white sword knot (officers' silver colored knot). Black leather scabbard tipped with silver, held by a white leather belt over the right shoulder.

TROOPER'S EQUIPMENT—Black leather ammunition waist pounch. A white carbine sling over the left shoulder with silver hook to support the gun. Carbin and pistol-wooden parts, red brown, metal parts silver except brass butt plate, trigger guard, ramrod guides and end stock cap.

OFFICER'S EQUIPMENT—A crimson waist sash, silver epaulets (field officers - epaulets on both shoulders, captains - right shoulder only, Subalterns - left shoulder only.)

TRUMPETER'S EQUIPMENT—A brass trumpet with red and dark blue twisted cording and tassels, carried over the left shoulder. Silver epaulets on both shoulders.

HORSE EQUIPMENT—Dark blue saddle cloth. Black holsters covered with black bearskin fur. Saddle - red brown or black leather, girth, buff. Harness, reins, headstall, breast strap, tail (crupper) strap and stirrup straps, black. Stirrup and bits silver. Picket rein - white.

HORSE COLORING—Usually (when obtainable) red brown or darker. Trumpeters rode white or light grays (when obtainable).

Finally, on 25 June, Colonel White was able to send a small squadron of sixty men to Lafayette. They had to be led by their troop commanders as White was so involved in trying to complete his Regiment that he did not have the opportunity to lead it during this campaign. Lafayette combined this one available mini-squadron with the remnants of Armand's Legion cavalry (some forty horsemen) and about fifty riflemen into a temporary *legion* under Major William McPherson. In this unit, the First Dragoons usually operated in advance of the outnumbered American forces, screening them and harassing the enemy.

Their first major action was on 26 July at Spencer's Ordinary against Simcoe's Queen's Rangers and some Hessian Jaegers, who had been collecting cattle and burning American supplies above

American Cavalry (of "Lee's Legion") under the command of
Henry "Light Horse Harry" Lee at Guilford.

Continental Remounts by W. Smithson Broadhead.

Williamsburg, Virginia. General Wayne, with Lafayette's approval, sent Colonel Richard Butler to intercept Simcoe. Butler marched all night, but still would have failed to overtake Simcoe, if McPherson had not pushed ahead with the cavalry, fifty of the best mounted Dragoons carrying light infantrymen up behind them. Simcoe was surprised, but rallied and held off his attackers long enough to escape after a fierce hand-to-hand fight.

Both sides claimed the victory. Their losses were about thirty men each. First Dragoon casualties included one captain wounded, five troopers killed, one trooper captured. The result of this affair was to make the British light troops somewhat less aggressive.

The next engagement was at Green Springs, where Cornwallis nearly succeeded in mousetrapping Lafayette's entire force. The First Dragoons were with the American advance guard at the beginning of the affair and intervened to cover Wayne's eventual retreat. Lafayette thanked them in his general orders for their gallant part in the action.

During the subsequent siege of Yorktown, the First Dragoons served with Lauzun's Legion on Gloucester Point, blockading the British forces there, which included their old foes, Tarleton's Legion and Simcoe's Legion.

CAMPAIGN OF 1782-1783

After the surrender of Cornwallis at Yorktown, the First Dragoons were sent to South Carolina to reinforce Greene, then blockading Charleston. Arriving on 4 January 1782, Lieutenant Colonel White was transferred to the command of the Fourth Continental Light Dragoons and Major John Swan succeeded him to the First Dragoons to command temporarily.

After a period of outpost duty around Charleston, the First Dragoons became a part of General Pickens' expedition to the Georgia frontier against an irregular band under a notorious Colonel Waters and the marauding Cherokees. Lieutenant Colonel White, who had returned after taking part in Wayne's successful Georgia campaign, resumed the command of the First Dragoons. Once in Cherokee territory, White was detached on 24 September

1782 to destroy the Indian villages along the Chattahoochee River, then rendezvous with Pickens for the attack on Waters' base. White rejoined that same afternoon after successfully carrying out his mission. Unfortunately, Waters had been forewarned in time to make his escape to the British stronghold of Saint Augustine, Georgia. However, an advantageous treaty was imposed upon the Cherokee tribes, and the First Dragoons returned to South Carolina late in October without the loss of a man.

This had been hard service, nevertheless, through the hot months of the year, and the First Dragoons had a long sick list when they returned to Greene's camp. They had made their campaign without tents or camp equipment. When the small ration of bread they could carry in their saddlebags was exhausted, they lived on parched corn, potatoes, peas, and beef collected in the Cherokee towns. There was no salt available.

On 9 November 1782 the First and Third Continental Light Dragoons were consolidated into five troops commanded by the released (from British captivity) Colonel George Baylor, the original commander and founder of the Third Dragoons, he was also the senior officer of the two Regiments. Major Swan held the actual command, the other field officers being either sick or on furlough.

After the British evacuated Charleston in December 1782, Major Swan with his own command and the Fourth Dragoons were stationed at Combahee to observe the British at Saint Augustine, as well as for greater convenience in securing forage. Here the American cavalry remained until the spring of 1783, the combined strength of the three regiments dwindling to 200 officers and men.

On hearing that peace had been declared, half of the dragoons placed a Sergeant Dangerfield at their head and deserted in a body, seizing the horses of those of their comrades who would not join them. They had enlisted only for the duration of the war and had not been paid for months, but by this mutiny they forfeited the pensions which they had so courageously earned at the cost of so many hardships. If they could have endured a few weeks longer they would have been included in the order to furlough the troops until the signing of the definite articles of peace. The dismounted dragoons of the three regiments, who had been left behind at James Island with the Continental infantry, fared better. In July the long awaited transports finally arrived and carried them northward to their homes.

Thus ended the career of "Bland's Horse", something of a personification of rugged American individualism. Posterity might well remember them for their tenacity to remain in existence to continue their part in carving our America's independence. Long re-told will be their exploits under "Light Horse Harry"; their charges under Pulaski, particularly at Savannah; their heroic service with Colonel Washington in Greene's army; their assault, riding double, at Spencer's Ordinary; and for their grueling service as Indian hunters against the Cherokees.

Part Two
SHELDON'S CONNECTICUT HORSE

THE SECOND CONTINENTAL LIGHT DRAGOONS

The Second Dragoons exceeded the personification of the ideal type of Dragoon. They not only fought and won victories on horse and foot but on the water as well. They were also the key to Washington's espionage service. None of the four Light Dragoon regiments surpassed Sheldon's Horse for uniquely active and effective service. Too little has been written of the impact that "Sheldon's Connecticut Horse" had in the American Revolution.

"Sheldon's Horse" (The Second Continental Light Dragoons) trace their lineage to the New York campaign of 1776 in the form of the Fifth Regiment of Connecticut Light Horse Militia. The Regiment was led by Major Elisha Sheldon, son of a Connecticut Legislator. Major Sheldon had served as an officer in the Connecticut Light Horse Militia since 1768. The 1776 Regiment consisted of seven mini-troops, the complete squadron comprising only 120 to 125 men.

The mini-squadron, it was hardly more than that, left Connecticut on 21 October, 1776, by order of the Governor to join Washington's army. They were the replacement unit for Major Backus's Connecticut Horse which Washington had diplomatically "released with thanks" after observing one of the Captains shaving a trooper on the parade grounds before his headquarters.

To 25 December, throughout the disheartening retreat through New Jersey in November and December, Sheldon's Horse were invaluable in their scouting and reconnaissance service while attached to Brigadier Rezin Beall's brigade. By the time Washington's army had reached the Delaware, Sheldon's squadron had disolved to a mere score of troopers, as the enlistments of most of the men had expired on December 25th.

Prior to this, impressed with the ability of Sheldon and his squadron, Washington sent Major Sheldon to the Continental Congress, then sitting at Philadelphia, with the following letter of recommendation:

"Washington to Congress, December 11, 1776

I can only say that the service of himself and his Troop, has been such as merits the warmest thanks of the public and deserves a handsome compensation for their trouble. From the experience I have had in this Campaign, on the Utility of Horse, I am convinced there is no carrying on the war without them, and I would therefore recommend the Establishment of one or more corps (in proportion to the number of Foot) in addition to those already raised in Virginia [Bland's Virginia Horse]. If Major Sheldon would undertaken the command of a Regiment of Horse on the Continental Establishment I believe he could very soon raise them and I recommend him as a man of activity and spirit from what I have seen of him."

The next day, 12 December 1776, Major Elisha Sheldon was promoted and commissioned Colonel-Commandant of a regiment of Horse on the Continental establishment to be raised by him in Connecticut.

Although the regiment was to be designated Sheldon's Second Continental Light Dragoons, it had the distinction of being the first Light Dragoon Regiment to be commissioned and raised on the Continental establishment. Consequently it was the *First* Regular Cavalry Regiment of the United States Continental Army.

Two veteran officers, Captain Epaphras Bull, who was one of the commando party under Arnold that captured Ticonderoga on 10 May, 1776, and Lieutenant Thomas Young Seymour with the score or more remnants of Sheldon's Connecticut (Militia) Horse (now Second Continental Light Dragoons *designate*) led the mini-remaining nucleous force in Sheldon's absence. With the Philadelphia City Troop they constituted the only cavalry with Washington's army that executed the brilliant strokes at Trenton and Princeton on 25 December. As they were conveyed across the Delaware the Dragoon horses shied and balked at the floating ice in the river. Upon landing, several horses were found too lame to walk from the enforced inaction while standing so long in the freezing wind. Those that could move were mounted and the others charged dismounted in the surprise attacks of Trenton and Princeton, to chalk up their first cavalry honours.

Meanwhile, Sheldon went to Connecticut to raise the balance of his Regiment. Arriving there Sheldon chose his officers, following as much as possible Washington's orders to pick men of fortune from reputable families, who were then approved by Washington before being commissioned. The officers recruited throughout Connecticut taking into the Regiment only young, light, active men. It was not hard to obtain recruits as service in the Dragoons was sought after, and men clambered to join the Regiment, which they wouldn't have done if it were a Foot corps.

The Dragoon privates were to receive twenty dollars bounty money and a uniform on entering the service, "and to receive regular pay monthly", a factor which soon separated the dedicated patriot troopers from the others, as monthly pay was seldom available. The pay of the officers and troopers of the Regiment was to be:

Colonel-Commandant	22 pounds	10 shillings monthly Continental
Major	18 pounds	
Captains	15 pounds	
Lieutenants	10 pounds	
Cornets	8 pounds	
Adjutants	10 pounds	
Surgeons	0 pounds	
Surgeon's Mate	0 pounds	
Quartermaster	5 pounds	
Sergeants	4 pounds	10 Shillings
Corporals	3 pounds	
Trumpeters	3 pounds	
Privates	2 pounds	10 Shillings

Each non-commissioned officer and private were to be furnished with a good horse, saddle, bridle and a carbine, broadsword (sabre) and pistols, together with other accouterments belonging to a Light Horseman, at the expense of the Continental Congress. Washington preferred that no stallions, mares, white or gray horses were bought. When he quickly learned that it was hard to fine horses of any sex or color, he was glad to see his Dragoons mounted on any serviceable mount. In 1777, the horses bought were usually trotters of a good size purchased for about one hundred dollars when the Continental dollar was still a credible exchange. Later, when the Continental dollar lacked any credibility, horses could not be bought, and it was found necessary to impress them.

The Regiment was to consist of 1 Colonel, 1 Lieutenant-Colonel, 1 Major, an Adjutant, a Surgeon and Surgeon's Mate, and six troops consisting of: 1 Captain, 1 Lieutenant, 1 Cornet, 1 Quartermaster, 2 Sergeants, 2 Corporals, 1 Trumpeter, 1 Farrier, and 34 Troopers, making a strength per troop of 44 rank and file. The total strength of each of the four Light Dragoon Regiments was established at 228 Rank and File, later it was increased on paper but never fully implemented in actuality.

Wethersfield, Connecticut was fixed as the rendezvous for the Second Continental Light Dragoons. All officers and recruits were ordered to assemble there. Benjamin Tallmadge, who was to bring such fame to the Regiment had received the first Captain's commission of the Second Dragoons and offered the command of the first troop to be raised. He arrived at Wethersfield and immediately erected a large circular "Manage" for the purpose of training and breaking the horses. During the winter and spring the recruits were broken into the Dragoon service and made acquainted with the routine and discipline of a Light Horseman. When the campaign of 1777 opened they were fairly well fit to take to the field, although most of the men had not as yet been under fire as a Dragoon.

The standards of the Regiment were quite similar to that of the Philadelphia City Troop, the difference being in the color, which was blue and gold for the Second. Captain Tallmadge's original troop had their own colors which were the same as the Regimental standard except for a red field. The motto on the two standards read: "The Country calls and her sons respond in thunder tones", inscribed in Latin.

Tallmadge did much to instill a marked esprit d' corps in the Regiment. His first troop was a shining example and the crack troop of the Regiment. His troopers were mounted entirely on dapple-gray horses, which, with black straps and black bear-skin holster-covers, looked superb. Tallmadge was proud of "this noble body of horse" and recorded the same in his Memoirs.

The other troops during the campaign of 1777 at least, were not as admirably fitted, and especially in the way of arms. As late as April 13, 1777, Colonel Sheldon writes that carbines "are making", he is buying pistols where he can, and has procured "steel for the sword blades", which, with the hilts are still "making". He adds that the business goes on slowly, as the manufacturers are entirely new in the business and prices are high.

As the men were recruited they were put on the roster which was kept throughout the war by Tallmadge. It is printed in the official "Record of Connecticut Men in the War of The Revolution", and is one of the most complete documents of its kind in our Revolutionary archives, as it gives not only all the names, dates of enlistment, promotion, discharge, etc., but the residence, occupations and casualties, and what is very uncommon, a descriptive list of the men, including their stature, complexion and color of eyes and

Major Benjamin Tallmadge
Second Continental Light Dragoons
From a watercolor portrait of 1945 by Helene Loescher

hair. This detailed *dossier* of each trooper gives one an insight into Tallmadge's later ability to become Washington's most successful espoinage chief in the Long Island sound area.

The rolls show that about seven hundred officers and men served in the Second Dragoons during the war. The Regiment never numbered over 250 effectives at any one time.

The uniform of the Second Continental Light Dragoons for 1777 was not the same throughout the six troops. Some troops wore brown coats faced with white, red or buff, white wool stockings, short gaiters or spatterdashes. Others wore blue coats faced with red. By October, 1777, Captain Thomas Y. Seymour's troop on the Saratoga front were the second best troop of the Regiment in the way of appointments. They wore a blue coat, buff leather breeches, black half boots, white cross belts. Their helmets at first were of leather with white horsehair crests, but later were of steel or brass, turned up at the base with brown bearskin and had long flowing white horse-hair crests. They were at first captured from the enemy and later imported from France after the alliance. The rest of the troops were in accordance in regard to the helmets.

In 1778 the rest of the Regiment adopted the same uniform of Captain Seymour's troop (when available) and wore it until the latter part of 1779. The Regiment was armed at first with only the saber and pistols, but after 1777 had in addition, carbines or short muskets with a sling. When not in use, the carbine was carried muzzle forward in a leather bucket attached to the right of the saddle.

By 1779 and through 1781 to the end of the war the general uniform and equipment of the Regiment was as follows:

HELMET—Brass, with black leather visor, white horse hair crest, medium blue turban.

HAIR—Natural color, tied with que ribbon in back. Powdered white for rare dress occasions.

NECK STOCK—Black.

COAT—Dark blue faced with buff on collar, lapes, cuffs and coat tail turnbacks. Brass buttons (Officers - gold color). To conform to the contemporary custom the trumpeters may have been dressed in reverse facings, viz., a buff coat with dark blue dollar, lapels, cuffs and coat tail turnbacks.

VEST—Buff.

BREECHES—Buff colored cloth or leather.

BOOTS—Polished black with silver spurs. Either half-boots, or the German knee-length. The former preferred when obtainable.

SABER AND BELT—Silver hilt with white sword knot (Officers - gold colored) held by a white leather belt over the right shoulder.

TROOPER'S EQUIPMENT—Black leather ammunition waist pounch. A white carbine sling over the left shoulder with silver colored hook to support the gun. Carbine and Pistol - wooden parts red brown, metal parts silver hued, except brass butt plate, trigger guard, ramrod guides and end stock cap.

OFFICER'S EQUIPMENT—A crimson waist sash and gold hued epaulets. Field officers (Colonels and Major) epaulets on both shoulders. Captain - right shoulder only. Subalterns (Lieutenants and Cornets) on left shoulder only.

TRUMPETER'S EQUIPMENT—A brass trumpet with buff and dark blue twisted cording and tassels, carried over the left shoulder. Gold epaulets on both shoulders.

HORSE EQUIPMENT—Dark blue saddle cloth. Black holsters covered with black bear fur. Saddle - red-brown or black. Girth - buff. Harness, reins, headstall, breast strap, tail (crupper) strap and stirrup straps, black. Stirrups and bits, silver hue. Also, a white picket rein.

HORSE COLORING—Red-brown or darker brown. Major Tallmadge's troop rode dapple grays. Trumpeters rode white or light grays when obtainable.

CAMPAIGN OF 1777

Spring of 1777 had arrived and Howe was stirring in New York and Washington was anxious to gather all of his forces about him as rapidly as possible. He ordered Colonel Sheldon to forward all recruits of his Second Dragoons as fast as they were collected. He also dispatched a particular order to send on all the effective men immediately. Sheldon had just enough men and horses to form two troops. They were accordingly put in the best order and the command of the squadron was given to Captain Tallmadge, he being the senior Captain in the Regiment. One of the troops was Tallmadge's crack dapple gray horse troop.

Directing their line of march by way of Farmington, Harrington, Litchfield, and Kent, in Connecticut, and from there to Peekskill and King's Ferry, where they crossed the Hudson River. From here to Haverstraw, the Clove, and Pompton to Morristown, where Washington had encamped his army the preceding winter. Reporting his arrival to Washington he ordered Tallmadge to move his detachment the next day to his encampment near Middlebrook, where he reviewed the squadron and commended Tallmadge on its excellent appearance.

The following day, all of the Light Horse then in Washington's camp, consisting of Bland's First Continental Light Dragoons, Moylan's Fourth Dragoons and Tallmadge's squadron of the Second were ordered to parade and proceed down to Woodbridge to reconnoitre the enemy. On 24 June, coming in sight of the advanced guard of the British, the enemy formed and tried to flank the American Dragoons on the right and left, while a strong party advanced to appear in their rear. The Dragoons, each squadron taking a separate course, charged through the enveloping circle. Suffering little loss, though they sustained a heavy fire from a much more numerous foe, the Dragoon retired in good order to headquarters and encamped being covered by Colonel Morgan's regiment of riflemen.

Four days later, on 28 June, the patrols came in, announcing the approach of the British. The dragoons were scarcely mounted when the enemy were in sight and the firing began, which inaugurated the Battle of Short Hills. The action, though indecisive, gave the Continental Light Dragoons preliminary fighting experience for the heavier battles later in the campaign. When Howe retired the Dragoons hovered upon his rear until they reached Elizabethtown. From there Howe drew in his out-posts, and the British fleet sailed from Sandy Hook on 23 July.

As soon as Washington knew definitely that Philadelphia was Howe's destination, he put his whole army in motion for the Delaware. The squadron of the Second Dragoons under Tallmadge marched southward by way of Carrol's Ferry over the Delaware.

Proceeding to Germantown the squadron joined Washington, who was anxiously awaiting to discover where Howe would land his army.

By this time more recruits for the Second had come on from Connecticut and the squadron was assuming a more corpulent appearance, so much so that Captain Tallmadge was promoted to Major. His commission dated from the time of the promotion of Major Samuel Blagden to Lieutenant Colonel on 7 April, 1777.

The Regiment served on three fronts in 1777. Besides Tallmadge's squadron with Washington, Colonel Sheldon had raised the other four troops and dispatched one of them under Lieutenant Thomas Y. Seymour to serve with Gates in the north. Though partially retarded by the heavily wooded country about Saratoga, Seymour's troop nevertheless distinguished themselves in the campaign, so much so that Seymour was promoted to Captain in October. Colonel Sheldon, with the remaining three troops served under General Putnam at Peeksville on the east side of the Hudson in 1777, to oppose a possible advance of Clinton up the Hudson from New York. They were also busy in harassing the Loyalists in the neighborhood and intercepting supplies they were smuggling into New York City.

The squadron with Major Tallmadge however, were actively engaged at Brandywine and in the Battle of Germantown they were at the head of General Sullivan's division on the left of the centre. In the thick fog the various division of the American army became confused and retreated when they could have had victory. Washington ordered Major Tallmadge to throw his squadron across the road to prevent the retiring American infantry, but to no avail. The squadron of the Second now galloped up and joined Brigadier General Pulaski, the new "Chief of the Dragoons", who was effectively covering the retreat of the American army with all the detachments of the Continental Light Dragoons that could be gathered.

The American army retired to Shippack and Howe returned to Philadelphia. Meanwhile Burgoyne had surrendered at Saratoga and Seymour's troop of the Second was released from that front to join Sheldon on the Hudson with the Saratoga Battle Honour brought with them to add to the Trenton and Princeton Honours.

32

Determined to engage Howe again before winter set in, Washington moved down to White Marsh and occupied the strong grounds on the north side of the flat ground known by that name. On the morning of 4 December, Howe came out of Philadelphia with the whole British army and encamped at Chestnut Hill, directly in front of the American right flank, then shifted later to the left flank on the end of which, Tallmadge was posted with his squadron, together with Morgan's Light Infantrymen and riflemen. They came in contact with the British Light Infantry and Dragoons (the 16th and 17th Light Dragoons). It appeared for a while that a general battle was inevitable, but neither General thought it wise to descend into the plain. After continuing in this position a few days, Howe retired to Philadelphia, much to Washington's amazement who now retired to Valley Forge for winter quarters.

As soon as the American army had encamped, Major Tallmadge was stationed with a strong detachment of the squadron, as an advanced corps of observation between Washington's army and that of the enemy. The detachment scoured the country from the Schuylkill to the Delaware River, about five or six miles, for the double purpose of watching the movements of the enemy and preventing the Loyalists from carrying supplies or provisions to Philadelphia. Their service was hard, and the weather was fierce. They were not able to linger long in any warm place, because of the British Light Horse, which continually patrolled the same ground. It was usually unsafe for Tallmadge to permit the Second Dragoons to unsaddle their horses for even an hour. Very rarely did the detachment stay in one place the same night.

One night while on this duty they were attacked at two o'clock in the morning by a large body of British Light Horse, under Lord Rawdon. As long as the action lasted on the road, the Second Dragoons put up a stubborn defense and were holding their own, but when the British Horse leaped the fences on the side of the road and got upon their flanks they were forced to retreat. Tallmadge's losses were comparitively small in this engagement. Four Dragoons were killed and as many wounded of the Second.

Soon after this action, Tallmadge was inadvertantly initiated into the espionage service by a surprisingly dramatic event. Tallmadge was informed that a country girl had gone into Philadelphia with eggs as her cover with instructions to obtain necessary information about the British there. Acting in concert, Tallmadge moved his detachment of Second Dragoons to Germantown where he left them. With a small party of them he advanced several miles toward the British lines. He dismounted at a tavern called The Rising Sun in full view of their outposts. He had not long to wait. Very soon a young attractive woman was seen coming out of the city. She came to the tavern, where she made herself known to Tallmadge and while she was giving him some important intelligence, they were hurriedly informed that the British Light Horse were coming. Stepping to the door, Tallmadge saw them chasing in his patrols, one of whom they managed to take prisoner. Quickly mounting his horse, the spy begged to go with him. Swinging her lithe body up behind his saddle they galloped up to Tallmadge's Second Dragoon rendezvous in Germantown, fighting off their pursuers with sword and pistols all the way, the American spy being an equal to Tallmadge and his meagre patrol in beating off their determined attackers. After an ardous running fight they managed to hold off their pursuers until they sighted Germantown where the Second Dragoon detachment there sighted the situation and galloped out to their rescue and drove off the British horse.

This caper so intrigued Major Tallmadge to the fascinating life of espionage that he soon was offering his services to Washington which would launch him on an incredible dual role as a famous Cavalry leader and Master Spy.

Tallmadge's duty on the lines before Philadelphia was over in January and he joined the rest of his squadron at Trenton, where Pulaski had been sent with all the American Dragoons, as a more accessible place for forage for the horses. From there the squadron of Second Light Dragoons was removed to Chatham, New Jersey for the remainder of the winter. Here they were permitted to rest from their hard and grueling service in the active but frustrating 1777 campaign. In the meantime, Colonel Sheldon had gone into winter quarters in Connecticut with the other squadron of the Second.

CAMPAIGN OF 1778

A parting farewell was flung at the Regiment by the British before the Second's exodus to New Jersey for better forage. Captain John Jameson was wounded in a skirmish near Valley Forge on 21 January, 1778. The wound could not have been too serious for Jameson was back at the game of petit warfare in February for he was reporting a gain over James DeLancey's Loyalist corps. And so it went, back and forth, the acquisition of Dragoon equipment, horses and horse fodder, being prime objectives for both sides.

Though primarily inactive militarily, the Dragoon commanders and field officers now conducted their never ending and most frustrating campaign of procurement of supply of clothing, food, arms, remounts and horse fodder. Colonel Sheldon recruited and "procured" in New York, New Jersey and particularly all of New England as Washington and Congress had stipulated that the resupply area for the Second Continental Light Dragoons was "east ward of the North [Hudson] River", which included New York and all of New England.

Washington's strategy was to eliminate the regimental competition in the four Dragoon regiments for procurement. His plan allowed each regiment to feret out supplies within their own familiar region. The Dragoon supply officer, Lt. Col. Samuel Blagden, for the Second Dragoons, should be familiar with his area manufacturers, their quality and reputation. His responsibility was great, as he was free of the army Quartermaster General, in his decision of procurement. Though his free rein was bridled by frequent and lengthy progress and detailed accounting reports to Washington. Boston, the principal free (of the British) New England port of the Second Dragoons supply sector, was Lt. Col. Blagden's goal in January. Here he encountered economic problems of a Bi-Centennial later, primarily inflation. There was a shortage of cavalry materials and price gouging by less than dedicated American patriot merchants. As a result there was a incredible inflationary rise in prices on which both military and civilian officials endeavoured to establish ceilings. Washington strove to fix a standard maximum average price per cavalry article. This would establish the top figure any cavalry officer including Blagden could bid. Blagden and others were ordered to keep this top bid price a secret so that any opportunist merchant would not demand the top price for items of dubious quality.

While most of the states established civilian price controls their lack of strong governmental control in most states made their effort unsuccessful. New Jersey was one of the exceptions.

Cooperation between the Military and Civilian authorities was frequently poor and the Dragoon procurement officers were unable to capitalize on the few existing price controls. Colonel Sheldon's dilemma was a case in point: — He agreed to purchase 140 leather breeches for his Second Dragoons at a fixed price, from a New Jersey tailor. Before delivery the State of New Jersey passed a lower price ceiling on this item. Major Tallmadge, Sheldon's Adjutant, aware of the lower established ceiling, attempted to pay the tailor the new lower price. Both parties appealed to Washington, who reluctantly acquiesed in favour of the tailor and his ". . . anterior Contract."

While in winter quarters at Chatham, Major Tallmadge attempted to re-equip his squadron of the Second for the forthcoming campaign. He wrote Washington of the difficulty of securing good remounts, and went into details of forage, recruits, etc. Although he found it almost impossible to obtain anything on credit, he succeeded in making a few contracts for equipment for his squadron, while Lieutenant Colonel Blagden in Boston concentrated more on Sheldon's squadron of the Second.

To one of Tallmadge's letters on the subject Washington replied on 20 February 1778, implying that he (Washington) was learning fast the army procurement strategy:

"I am glad to be informed by your letter of the 9th instant that you are established in uarters where you are likely to have means of putting your men and horses into good condition; as you have been so successful in contracting for boots and leather breeches, I would not have you confine your views in these articles to the precise number that may be wanted by your Regiment, but wish that you would extend them in such a manner as to be useful to the other Regiments [of Dragoons].

The sums which may be wanted to fulfil your agreement must be drawn from the Quarter master General in whose hands a fund is established for defraying all expenses of this kind.

It gives me pain that there should be any delay in the important business of providing Remounts; this matter among others is under the consideration of the Committee of Congress now in Camp, and nothing can be done in it till their determination is known".

On 10 March, 1778, Washington again penned Tallmadge:

"As Congress has called upon those States in which there is the best breed of Horses, to furnish a supply for the Cavalry, I cannot take upon me to put money into Colonel Sheldon's hands for the purchase of remounts for his Regiment in particular, which will be provided for among the rest; at the same time if he can engage some good horses at reasonable prices on credit, I will promise that they shall be paid for hereafter. I have no doubt that Colonel Sheldon will be able to enlist a number of men for the established Continental bounty, as the service of the cavalry is sought by many who will not engage in the Infantry."

In spite of all this rhetoric of promises of sustainment of the Dragoons, Tallmadge had to rely on his personal funds for credit to keep his squadron of men and horses from starving. He was forced to remain in debt for over a year before he was reimbursed.

During their winter cantonment, apparently several of the officers of the four Dragoon Regiments took it upon themselves to absent themselves without leave, to visit their homes, or for various other diversions, much to the wear and tear of their mounts. The Second Dragoons officers with Tallmadge, were no exception and the irate Washington expressed himself to Tallmadge as follows:

"Valley Forage 13th May, 1778

I received your favor of the 4th instant by Colonel Sheldon.

I do not censure the conduct of officers or hurt their feelings in the smallest degree through choice. When I do it, I always regret the occasion which compelled me to the measure.

How far the conduct of the generality, or of Individual officers in your Corps may have been reprehensible and deserving the reproof and charges contained in my letter, I cannot determine upon my own knowledge. I shall be happy if they were without foundation.

*However, my information was such that I could not dis-
believe the facts. It came through various channels and it
appeared that the horses had been neglected and greatly
harassed. Colonel Moylan [now Brigade-Major of the four
Dragoon Regiments] in his general report of the state of the
cavalry informed me 'That the Second Regiment had been
cruelly dealt with, of 54 horses which he had seen paraded that
he did not think Ten could be selected to go on any duty. That
they had been starved during the winter and the blame thrown
from the officers on Mr. Caldwell, who acted as a Commissary
of the Forage, but that the true reason of their being in such
condition, according to his belief, was that few or none of the
officers had been with the Regiment.' If this was the case —
If the horses were neglected in their absence or not attended to
as well as circumstances would admit, the officers are certainly
reproachable for not having done that duty they owed the
Public."*

Early in the spring, the enemy, making some movements on the
Hudson, Tallmadge's squadron was ordered to leave their winter
quarters at Chatham and proceed towards the Clove and King's
Ferry to watch their motions. Major Tallmadge received his marching orders from Washington the latter part of May, to report with
his two troops to General Gates commanding the middle department on the Hudson. On 1 June Tallmadge wrote Gates, then at
Robinson's House, that he would start from Chatham as soon as he
could mount all his men. He expressed pleasure at "The prospect
of seeing the Regiment once together which has not happened since
we have been raised."

Consequently, Tallmadge's squadron was not present at Monmouth, just missing the opportunity to engage in the battle by
about ten days. However, before joining Gates, he was ordered to
temporarily re-join Washington's army after the battle at White
Plains.

Meanwhile, Colonel Sheldon, with the other squadron had left
winter quarters in Connecticut to return to the Hudson front. Here
Tallmadge joined him with his squadron. Captain Seymour and his
troop returned from the north with the Saratoga victory under their

belts. Here, in August, 1778, the Second Continental Light Dragoons assembled for the first time as a unit under Colonel Sheldon. For eighteen months the Regiment had been separated, but they had the honor of serving in three distinct important spheres of operations in the campaign of 1777, and at the union of the three detachments the men felt and were, like seasoned veterans. Their ability had been rewarded. Particularly, the exemplary conduct of Captain Tallmadge promoted to Major. Lieutenant Thomas Y. Seymour elavated to a Captaincy three days after Burgoyne's Surrender, for Seymour's distinguished service in the Saratoga campaign.

Sheldon's Second Continental Light Dragoons were now ordered down to the Westchester lines and joined General Scott's Light Corps.

After the battle of Monmouth and the retreat of the British army to New York City, Westchester County became very active again. The Queen's Rangers under Simcoe and other Loyalist Corps, a troop of Light Horse under Emmerick, and Delancey's battalions, now became active in patroling and foraging in lower Westchester. To oppose their incursions. Scott, with his American Light Corps and Sheldon's Light Horse, took post on the Greenburg Hills, and extended his left toward New Rochelle. Sometimes Sheldon's Second Dragoons advanced as far as Valentines Hill, which was a favorite camp ground for both sides during the war, and the foraging parties of the enemy were stymied. Frequent and bloody skirmishes ocurred between the Second and the Loyalist Light Horse and the most vigilant and wary were the most successful. Here, in this locality Sheldon's main body of Second Dragoons with infantry supports guarded the same ground to the close of the war, earning for themselves the name of "The Watchdogs of the Highlands".

Washington had no complaints of his Dragoons as long as they were scoring the highest. However, he was greatly chagrined when a patrol of Sheldon's Horse were surprised on the Clap Tavern Road on the morning of 7 October 1778 with a loss of nine Dragoons and eleven horses. He immediately penned a letter to Colonel Sheldon to relay the following threat to his officers:

"If any officer regardless of his own reputation and the important duty he owes the public, suffers himself to be sur-

prised, he cannot expect if taken, that interest should be made for his exchange, or if he saves his person, to escape the Sentence of a Courtmartial."

The year 1778 saw the advent of Major Tallmadge's entry into the vital espionage service in which he so distinguished himself with members of the Second Dragoons in their amazing performance of these more subtle services. Tallmadge launched the beginning of his intricate espionage by opening a private correspondence with agent Robert Townsend, code name "Samuel Culper, Junior", in New York City, to supply vital information to Washington on the movements of the British in New York City. Secret invisible ink perfected in England was smuggled to America and penned between the lines of innocent communications from "Culper" to Tallmadge. Though lacking the sophistication of modern electronic espionage devices, still Tallmadge's methods were most effective for the times. His secret service became the eyes of Washington's secret reconnaissance of Clinton's movements in and out of New York. Tallmadge was so indispensable that Washington maintained him as his Secret Service chief (anonymous) of the Long Island Sound for the duration of the war. Tallmadge kept one or more boats continually employed in crossing the Sound on this espionage service.

When the campaign of "78" closed, the Second Dragoons went to Durham, Connecticut for winter quarters. Part of the Regiment was kept continually active throughout the cold winter. Sheldon was instructed to keep a patrol of a non-com and six Dragoons patrolling in the southeastern corner of Connecticut to prevent the Loyalists smuggling activities. The patrol was frequently changed for this hard service. This procedure was followed during each winter for the remainder of the war.

Part of the winter, Tallmadge with his Second Dragoon "agents" were, from choice, stationed at Greenfield near the Sound, from where he could easily cross to Long Island on their espionage service.

CAMPAIGN OF 1779

The spring of 1779 found the Second Light Dragoons back on the Westchester front and stationed at Poundridge.

In order to augment the Regiment to full strength, men had been enlisted to serve the length of the war and on foot until, "it shall be thought proper or convenient to mount them", and they were to be natives of Connecticut, "of good connection and character and in every way qualified for the Dragon sercie". According to a letter from Washington to Colonel Sheldon dated 14 August, 1779, the bounty was $200 per man (Continental paper money). It was found necessary to do this, owing to the difficulty of obtaining suitable horses to mount the whole Regiment. Due to the worthlessness of the Continental money the farmers would not sell their horses. About two troops of the Regiment were formed into dismounted Dragoons which was actually a function of the true *Dragoon* to be able to serve afoot as well as ahorse.

Not long after they took to the field in "79", the Regiment was engaged in a fierce action with Tarleton and his Legion. On the night of the 2nd of July, Lieutenant-Colonel Tarleton, with 360 of his Legion, Horse and Foot, came out from Mile Square and attacked a strong detachment of Sheldon's Second Dragoons, who were posted at Major Lockwood's home in Poundridge. The onset was violent and the conflict carried on principally with the sabre, until Tarleton's Legion infantry closed in the Second's flanks and the superior force forced the Second Dragoons, at first to retreat; but, being reinforced by American militia, they, in turn, pursued the enemy who had retired after burning Major Lockwood's house. A severe engagement took place in which Tarleton was driven off and four of his Legion taken prisoners. In this action the Second Dragoons had one Corporal, one Trumpeter, and eight privates wounded; three Sergeants, one Corporal, and four privates missing, and twelve horses missing. One of them was Major Tallmadge's blooded charger. In the saddle bags were most of Tallmadge's field baggage and twenty guineas in cash. The British claimed that they took one of the Regiments standards that had been left in the house when the Dragoons hurriedly turned out to engage with Tarleton. The British lost one killed, four taken prisoners and four horses.

Soon after this, the Second Dragoons were joined by Moylan's Fourth Continental Light Dragoons and the two Regiments frequently operated together for almost a year until June 1780, when Moylan's Dragoons left the Westchester front.

When Tyron made his raid into Connecticut, about a week after the Second Dragoons engagement with Tarleton at Poundridge, the Second and Fourth Dragoons were ordered to assist the militia at Norwalk in an expected invasion of that town. Tyron had landed and was driving back the militia when they arrived. The Dragoons covered their retreat and also that of the refugee families of the town which was burned by the raiders. Tyron's force was of such numbers that this was all the effective work the Second and Fourth Continental Dragoons could accomplish.

Returning to the Westchester front, the Second Dragoons, as part of Brigadier-General Robert Howe's army on the east side of the Hudson, on 15 July, moved up in view of the fort on Verplank's Point, as if to attack it, then retired and advanced again. Howe kept this up to divert the attention of the garrison from Stony Point across the River which was carried that night by General Wayne.

On August 5, a raid was planned in retaliation for Tyron's brutal Norwalk Raid. About 100 Light Horse of Sheldon's and Moylan's, Militia and about 40 Infantry of Glover's brigade, all under the command of Lieutenant-Colonel Anthony Walton White of the Fourth Dragoons, penetrated boldly within the British lines near Lower Salem. They successfully attacked a detachment of De-Lancey's Loyalist Brigade at their headquarters in a house at Morrisania. Taking them by surprise, 30 or more of this Loyalist corps were taken before the rest escaped. Considerable plunder was taken, including livestock. DeLancey's Corps rallied and with considerable reinforcements caught up with White's raiding party and attacked them. White fell back with his detachment of the Second and Fourth Dragoons and sustained a vigorous rear guard action with spirit, while his infantry reached the American lines safely with the prisoners and plunder. The British losses in the action were heavy in killed and wounded. White lost two killed and two wounded. After this audacious raid, DeLancey was forced to establish his headquarters near High Bridge, closer to New York City, and under the guns of a fort. General Washington thanked

White and his detachment for their gallant behaviour, particularly in their Dragoon rearguard action, and communicated their success to Congress.

Sheldon's and Moylan's Second and Fourth Dragoons, Armand's Legion and Glover's Brigade, were stationed at Lower Salem for the rest of the "79" campaign and there was hardly a day went by that parties of one or more of the above Corps did not engage with the partisan forces of the enemy. Major Tallmadge was to lead a detachment of the Second Dragoons in an expedition into Westchester. The enemy got wind of it and he was nearly led into an ambuscade. They threw a large body of infantry into a thicket on the side of the road, but Tallmadge received knowledge of the movement just before his Dragoons reached the spot and he retired in time without loss. On the way back to the Regiment's camp they were fired upon by sniping Loyalist "Cow Boys". Sergeant-Major James Dole, of Tallmadge's squadron was shot. The bullet entered through one of the hips and came out on the other side passing completely through his body. As soon as Tallmadge saw the wound he thought his veteran Sergeant was finished; but Dole recovered and served conspicuosly in the Regiment to the close of the War.

Before the "79" campaign closed the Second Dragoons effected one of their most brilliant exploits by attacking and capturing a large band of marauders at their stronghold at Fort Franklin on Lloyd's Neck. Lloyd's Neck was an elevated promontory between Oyster Bay and Huntington Harbor on Long Island. It was a strong position, and the fort covered the operations of wood-cutters for miles around. The garrisson consisted of 500 troops and in the rear of Fort Franklin just outside of its walls a large band of marauders encamped, who, having boats at their command, continually infested the Sound and the American shores. Determined to break up this band of freebooters or "pirates", Tallmadge left Shippan Point, near Stamford, Connecticut, on September 5, with one hundred and thirty Second Dragoons, dismounted. Reminiscent of Major Rogers' methods on Lakes George and Champlain in the French and Indian War, Tallmadge crossed the sound in whaleboats after dark, and at ten o'clock that night loosened the carbines at their thighs and attacked the much superior force of Tory marauders in their quarters. The daring attack was so sudden and unexpected, that they succeeded in capturing almost the whole band. A few escaped into the bushes and gave the alarm, thus preventing Tallmadge from attacking the outposts and guards of Fort Franklin.

After destroying all of the boats that could be found, as well as the huts of the "pirates", the Second Dragoons returned to their whaleboats with their prisoners and embarked for Connecticut, where they landed in safety and triumph before sunrise the next morning without the loss of a single Dragoon.

Besides breaking up the nest of Pirates, Tallmadge's daring stroke resulted in Lieutenant-Colonel Simcoe and his Loyalist Queen's Rangers fortifying their cantonment at Oyster Bay that winter, even though the Queen's Rangers numbered 360 strong at this time.

In October, 1779, Washington, in General Orders authorized a new uniform for the four Dragoon Regiments. The order stated that they were to be clothed in "all blue, faced with white; with white buttons and linings, and black half boots". As previously noted, the uniform was very much the same as the Second Continental Light Dragoons had been wearing. The "all blue" apparently meant that all of the four Regiments of Dragoons were to wear blue coats. A General Order for a uniform designation was one thing, but to be able to comply was another, it is doubtful that the four Regiments were able to all procure "blue coats".

At the close of the "79" campaign Sheldon's Dragoons wintered with Moylan's in Connecticut. The Second Dragoons were quartered at North Hampton for the winter. The men were paid entirely with next to worthless Continental paper money. The same exchange that had to procure food and clothing and forage. As a result these vital necessities were scarce and very difficult to come by.

Major Tallmadge was appointed to meet the Commissioners of the State of Connecticut at Weathersfield, to adjust and settle the depreciation of the pay of their troops, but very little good seems to have come from the meeting and the winter was an extremely hard one for the Regiment. The Regiment on 22 February 1780 showed a return of 1 Trumpeter, 1 Farrier, and 5 Troopers of "mounted effective Dragoons", out of six troops. The reasons given were

"Horses much reduced, almost a complete lack of necessary accoutrements, boots and other clothing." In March, Colonel Sheldon managed to get an order on Boston for the necessary clothing needed. This was irregular because he had no authority to take such action, as it was believed such liberty would be deranging the system for establishing the procurement of clothing for the American army. The Regiments were required to wait until Congress or the Regiment's State Government saw fit to send clothing and supplies. If Colonel Sheldon was aware of this he still was not going to see his troopers near naked through the cold winter. As a result of Sheldon's efforts to clothe his practically naked Dragoons he became involved in several law suits and in the late summer of 1780 he was even detained in gaol for a time, notwithstanding the fact that his own father was a member of the Connecticut Legislature.

CAMPAIGN OF 1780

In the spring the Regiment returned to the Westchester front establishing headquarters at North Castle.

The Second Dragoons now consisted of four mounted troops and two troops of dismounted Dragoons, who operated as Light Infantry. During the course of the summer Washington ordered Major Talmadge to serve with a few select Second Dragoon "Agents" to serve on detached duty at North Stamford, where they could keep an eye on the enemy, either up on the lines, or across the Sound on Long Island. Tallmadge's total command consisted of a troop of the mounted Second Dragoons and the two Light Infantry companies of the Regiment. The other three mounted troops remained with Colonel Sheldon on active duty at North Castle.

While at North Stamford, Tallmadge, determined to re-visit the scene of his successful whaleboat commando raid on Lloyd's Neck. He was about to lead his expedition across the Sound and attack the enemy's Fort Franklin on Lloyd's Neck, when his espionage service warned him that the enemy had received intelligence of his plan and a strong force was awaiting his arrival at the proposed place of landing. Tallmadge wisely abandoned the expedition.

Shortly after this, Major Tallmadge returned to the lines in

Westchester with his squadron.

In September, while Colonel Sheldon was detained in Salem gaol and courts over the winter clothing caper, Lieutenant Colonel Jameson was temporarily in command. At this time the Regiment played a conspicuos part in the Andre-Arnold case. Major Andre, in the guise of a merchant was on his way from the British to General Arnold in command of the strategic West Point, to receive plans of the fortifications and strength of the American forces there. He was intercepted by rebel farmers and taken before Jameson at North Castle. The farmers had searched Andre and found papers in his stockings. Jameson was suspicious, but since Andre had a pass from Arnold, Jameson kept the papers dispatching them to Washington and sent Andrew onwards with an escort under Lieutenant Allen.

Major Tallmadge, next in command to Jameson, was on duty below White Plains that day and did not return until evening. When informed of the circumstances, he was filled with astonishment at Jameson's mistake, and boldly expressed his suspicions of Arnold. He offered to take upon himself the entire responsibility of proceeding on that ground, if Jameson would let him. But Jameson refused to sanction any action that should imply a distrust of Arnold. Major Tallmadge then begged to have Andre brought back. To this Jameson reluctantly assented.

Jameson sent a courier after Lieutenant Allen, who brought Major Andre back. As soon as Tallmadge saw Andre, and observed his manner and gait while pacing the room, he was convinced that he was a military man; in the meanwhile Colonel Jameson had sent a courier with a letter to Arnold telling him why the prisoner was not sent to him. This is the letter that Benedict Arnold received in time to make his escape.

Andre was escorted by Major Tallmadge to Tappan, the headquarters of the Commander-in-Chief at that time. There, after Washington had completed arrangements for the security of West Point, he summoned a board of General Officers and they determined that Major Andre was indeed a spy. Finding him guilty, he was executed the next morning. While under Tallmadge's custody to the time of his execution, a friendship evolved between them. Though well liked by everyone, including Washington, still Andre could not be exchanged for Benedict Arnold. General Clinton, on his honor, could not turn Arnold over after his escape to the British.

Shortly after the Andre affair, Benedict Arnold was authorized by General Clinton to raise his "American Legion" of Horse and Foot. Arnold attempted to enlist several officers already serving in the Continental Army for the personnel of his new corps. Aware of the great ability of Major Tallmadge, he even attempted to secure his services, as can be seen by the following letter to him:

> "As I know you to be a man of sense, I am convinced you are by this time fully of opinion that the real interest and Happiness of America consists in a reunion with Great Britain. To which effect I have taken a commission in the British Army, and invite you to join me with as many men as you can bring over with you. If you think proper to embrace my offer, You shall have the same Rank you now hold in the Cavalry I am about to raise. I shall make use of no arguments to convince you, or to induce you to take a step which I think right. Your own good sense will suggest anything I can say on the subject. I will only add that the English Fleet has just arrived with a very large Reinforcement of Troops.
>
> B. Arnold, New York, October 25th, 1780, To Major Tallmadge."

Tallmadge ignored the letter and forwarded it to General Washington. A Psychologist could undoubtedly explain Arnold's motives in trying to seduce Washington's most able officers away from him: It would ease his own guilt if he could find kindred spirits. After Andre's execution, Major Tallmadge returned to his Second Dragoon detachment on the Westchester front.

The rest of the autumn of 1780 was spent by Sheldon's Light Horse in intercepting supplies intended for the British in New York and in skirmishes with the Loyalist "Cow Boys", in the Neutral ground in Westchester, located about 27 miles above New York City near Tarrytown. This was the haunt of the "Cow Boys", and the "Skinners", who infested the Neutral ground and made it a political and social hell for the inhabitants. Many left it, suffering their lands and homes to fall in ruins rather than remain in the midst of perpetual torments. The "Cow Boys" were mostly refugees belonging to the British side, and engaged in plundering the people near the lines, taking their cattle and driving them to New York, thus the name "Cow Boy". The "Skinners" professed attachment to the American cause and lived mostly within the Rebel lines; but they were of easy virtue, and were really more detested by the Americans than the Cow Boys. They were threacherous, rapacious, and often brutal. One day they would be engaged in Skirmishes with the Cow Boys, the next day they would be in league with them in plundering their own friends, as well as enemies. They were the fore-runners of similar so-called "partisan" bands that cropped up in all subsequent American wars. Often a sham skirmish would take place between them near the British lines; the Skinners were always victorious, and then they would go boldly into the interior with their booty, pretending it had been captured from the enemy while attempting to smuggle it across the lines. The profits from the sales were divided between the parties.

The Neutral ground, was a populous and highly cultivated region, about thirty miles in extent along the Hudson, covering nearly all of WestChester County, and between the American and British lines. Being within neither, it was called the Neutral ground. The inhabitants suffered terribly during the war, for they were certain to be plundered and abused by one party or the other. If they took the oath of fidelity to the American cause, the Cow Boys were sure to plunder them; if they did not, the Skinners would call them Tories (Loyalists), seize their property, and have it confiscated by the State.

It fell upon the Second Continental Light Dragoons to remedy this deplorable situation as much as possible and throughout the War the Regiment was unrelenting in their tracking down and destroying of these various bands of banditti.

In October, it looked like the Second Dragoons would see heavy action when word came in that the enemy were planning a large foraging drive as far up as Crom Pond and its vicinity, to sweep off all of the cattle. General Heath who commanded in the Highlands, ordered Colonel Hazen (the ex-Rogers Ranger Captain in the French and Indian War), with 500 men of his "Congress's Own" Regiment, to move to Pine's Bridge; and Lieutenant-Colonel Jameson, with the Second Dragoons, to move from Bedford toward

Hazen. Arriving at Pine Bridge on the night of 21 October, the two Regiments lay in ambush, but the British apparently were forewarned as they did not venture from their lines. In spite of the lack of action, this movement saved the Americans the loss of their cattle.

Before the end of 1780 Major Tallmadge made another brilliant coup to bolster American morale and make exciting reading in the Colonial press: A considerable body of Rhode Island Loyalist refugees had taken possession of the manor house of General John Smith at Smith's Point on the Atlantic side of Long Island. They fortified it and the grounds around it and began cutting wood for the British army in New York. At the solicitation of the American patriot, General Smith, and with the approval of Washington, Major Tallmadge, the "Long Island Raider", proceeded to dislodge them on the night of 21 November. The refugees had named their fortress, Fort St. George, and were too strongly entrenched to be in fear of an attack, especially at this late season.

Tallmadge had long eyed this expedition and he had planned carefully for it. Putting his Intelligence Department to work he obtained a plan of Fort St. George. To assure himself of the lay of the land, he went under cover, crossed the Sound, and made his own plan of the now completed Fort.

Satisfied with his completed reconnaissance he returned to the Connecticut shore to embark eighty picked dismounted Second Dragoons in whaleboats at four o'clock in the afternoon of the 21st. Crossing Long Island Sound from Fairfield, in the wake of a storm, they landed at Woodville. Because of the storm, they remained at Woodville throughout the remainder of the night and the next day, keeping themselves well hidden. The following night, November 22, Tallmadge and his Dragoons marched toward Fort St. George. At the mills, about two miles from the Fort, Tallmadge obtained a faithful guide, William Booth, who lived near the mills. General Smith's wife was also there, as she had been driven from her home. When Tallmadge told her he might have to destroy her house, she quickly replied, "Do it and welcome, if you can drive out those Tories".

At dawn, Tallmadge and his veteran Dragoons burst through the stockade on the southwestern side, rushed across the parade, and shouting the watchword, "Washington and Glory", they furiously assailed the redoubt upon three sides. The garrisson surrendered without resistance. At that moment a volley was fired from the upper window of the mansion. The outraged Dragoons, burst open the doors and would have killed every inmate for their treachery had not Major Tallmadge stopped them. Having secured the prisoners, consisting of the Commandant, a Lieutenant-Colonel, one Captain, one Lieutenant, one Surgeon and fifty rank and file, they destroyed the Fort, and burned the vessels lying at the wharf, which were on the verge of having their anchors lifted to make their escape with the valuable stores on board. Fort St. George was intended as a depository of stores for the Loyalists of Suffolk County. Tallmadge and his Dragoons, with the prisoners laden with the more valuable articles of dry goods, which had been removed from the vessels, set out at sunrise for their return march. On the way, Major Tallmadge left Captain David Edgar in command of the detachment, and mounting Sergeant Elijah Churchill and ten Dragoons on the horses taken at Fort St. George, started out with them for the town of Corum nearby. Tallmadge's espionage had revealed the maintenance of a huge forage supply dump for British cavalry. The destruction (or obtainment of) was a constant tactical objective by one and all of Washington's four Dragoon Regiments. Arriving undetected, they overpowered the guard and destroyed three hundred tons of hay collected for the British 17th Light Dragoons stationed at Hempstead, Long Island. After this exploit, they rejoined Captain Edgar at Woodville. Dragging their whale-boats from hiding Tallmadge embarked with his commando Dragoons and arrived safely at Fairfield, Connecticut, early in the evening without the loss of a single Dragoon in their three day excursion. The enemy losses at Fort St. George were 7 killed and wounded, besides the 53 prisoners taken. This brilliant expedition drew plaudits from Washington and the following high praise from the Continental Congress:

"In Congress, December 6th, 1780.
While Congress are sensible of the patriotism, courage and perseverance of the officers and privates of their regular forces, as well as of the militia throughout the United States, and of the military conduct of the principal Commanders in both, it

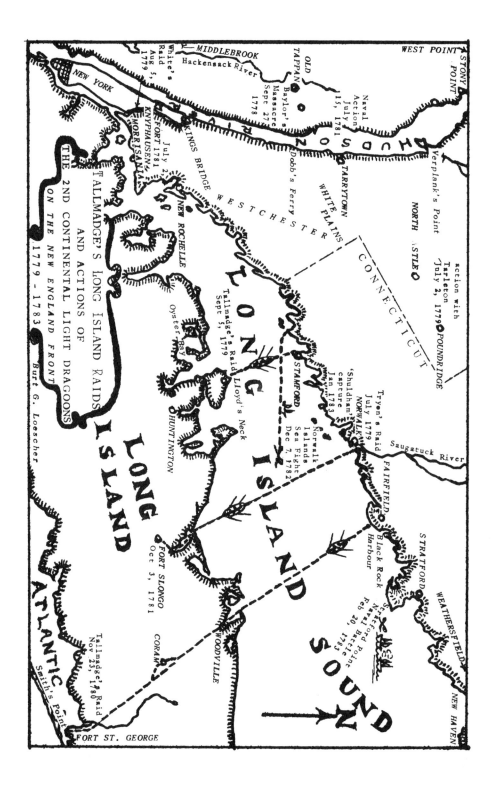

TALLMADGE'S LONG ISLAND RAIDS AND ACTIONS OF THE 2ND CONTINENTAL LIGHT DRAGOONS ON THE NEW ENGLAND FRONT 1779-1783

Burt G. Loescher

WEST POINT
STONY POINT

MIDDLEBROOK
Hackensack River

OLD TAPPAN
NEW YORK

White's Raid Aug 5, 1779

Baylor's Massacre Sept 27 1778

Naval Action July 15, 1781

Verplank's Point

North Castle

action with Tarleton July 2, 1779 POUNDRIDGE

KNYPHAUSEN'S MORRISANIA FORT 1781 July 2, 1781

KINGS BRIDGE

Dobb's Ferry

TARRYTOWN WHITE PLAINS

WESTCHESTER

NEW ROCHELLE

CONNECTICUT

Oyster Bay

LONG ISLAND

Tallmadge's Raid: Lloyd's Neck Sept 5, 1779

STAMFORD

HUNTINGTON

Tryon's Raid July 1779

NORWALK
Norwalk Islands Sea Fight Dec 7, 1782

'Shuldham' capture Jan. 1783

Saugatuck River

FAIRFIELD

LONG ISLAND

LONG ISLAND

FORT SLONGO Oct 3, 1781

Black Rock Harbour

STRATFORD

Nicford Point Naval Battle Feb 20 1783

WEATHERSFIELD

NEW HAVEN

ATLANTIC

Smith's Point

FORT ST. GEORGE

Tallmadge's Raid Nov 23, 1780

CORAM

WOODVILLE

SOUND

gives them pleasure to be so frequently called upon to confer marks of distinction and applause for the enterprises which do honour to the profession of arms and claim a high rank among military achievements. In this light they view the enterprise against Fort St. George, on Long Island, planned and conducted with wisdom and great gallantry by Major Tallmadge, of the Light Dragoons, and executed with intrepidity and complete success by the officers and soliders of his detatchment.

Ordered, therefore, That Major Tallmadge's report to the Commander-in-Chief be published, with the preceding minute, as a tribute to distinguished merit and in testimony of the sense Congress entertains of this brilliant service."

Of all of Major Tallmadge's Long Island expeditions, the capture of Fort St. George was the most brilliant and was equal to Light Horse Harry Lee's capture of Paulus Hook. Unlike Lee, Tallmadge had no reinforcements to fall back on. From the time he embarked from Connecticut with his Dragoons, they were on their own and subject to the mercy of the capricious weather in the twenty mile stretch of water in the Sound between Fairfield and Woodville. While they were attacking Fort St. George on the distant Atlantic side, there was the possibility of roving parties of the enemy finding their hidden whaleboats (shades of Rogers' expedition to destroy St. Francis in 1759) which would have left them trapped on Long Island. Tallmadge's tactics and daring had echoes of the famous Ranger.

Returning to the Westchester front, Tallmadge and his squadron remained actively engaged with the rest of the Second Dragoons until late December, when the Regiment withdrew to Simsbury and Windsor in Connecticut for winter quarters.

CAMPAIGN OF 1781

When the Second Continental Light Dragoons took to the field for the campaign of '81, they were on a new establishment. Although the Regiment had actually existed since August, 1779, in a Legionary form, that is, Horse and Foot, they were now officially ordered to put themselves on a Legion footing by Washington and the Continental Congress as follows:

> *"On November 1, 1780: the following organization of the American Cavalry to take effect January 1, 1781:*
>
> *Four Regiments of Cavalry or Light Dragoons or Legionary Corps, to consist each of four troops of mounted Dragoons and Two of dismounted Dragoons, that each troop consist of 60 privates and the same number of commissioned and non-commissioned officers as at present. The terms of enlistment for the war only."*

Although this authorization fixed the strength of the Dragoon Regiments at 360 men, the Second Dragoons, as well as the other three Regiments, never exceeded 250-275 effectives at any one time. There were never over 150-200 of these in each Regiment that were mounted Dragoons.

The campaign of 1781 opened vigorously for the Second Dragoons. When the French army, marching from New England in the summer of 81' approached the Hudson, Washington was informed that a large detachment of British troops had left New York for a marauding expedition into New Jersey. Washington had long cherished a desire to drive the enemy from Manhattan Island and now there appeared a favorable opportunity to strike Fort Knyphausen at King's Bridge. The Fort was the key to the British fortifications at New York. Arrangements were made to begin the attack on the night of 2 July, 1781, believing Rochambeau would arrive with the French army by that time. Part of the plan was to cut off the Second Dragoons' old foe, DeLancey's Loyalist corps along the Harlem River. This enterprise was intrusted to the Duke de Lauzun, with his Legion, which was approaching, and Sheldon's Second Dragoons and Continental Infantry were to be attached to Lauzun's force. An American force approaching the Fort was discovered and fired upon. Lauzun's presence was now revealed before his Legion Hussars and Sheldon's Horse could come up to DeLancey. DeLancey at Fort No. 8, ever alert, since the Second Dragoons surprise attack on his former Morrisania Headquarters, heard the firing and retreated to Fort Knyphausen in time. The British sallied out in force upon Lincoln's force who had approached the Fort. Lauzun and Sheldon, coming up with their Light Horse, engaged the British and sustained a spirited rear-guard action while Lincoln retired with his Continental Infantry. Further attempts on Fort Knyphausen were abandoned as the British fell back to it.

Washington withdrew to Dobbs' Ferry, where he was joined by Rochambeau on 6 July. He reconnoitred the enemy lines with Rochambeau under the protection of strong detachments of the Second Dragoons and Lauzun's Hussars.

The Second Dragoons were again engaged in a martime coup on the evening of 15 July. Two sloops of war, two tenders, and one galley, of the British fleet, went up the Hudson with the intention of destroying the supplies, then moving from West Point to the American army. At that time there were two sloops going down the River, laden with cannon and powder. As soon as they discovered the British, they put about and headed in for Tarrytown, where they ran aground. The British, having a good wind and tide, came up the river so fast that it was impossible to march infantry down in time to unload or protect the stores, as there were no troops at Tarrytown, except a Sergeant's guard of French Infantry. The Second Dragoons were encamped at Dobbs Ferry at the time and Colonel Sheldon immediately ordered his Dragoons to mount and dashed up to Tarrytown with them. Upon arriving, Sheldon and his Dragoons dismounted and feverishly assisted in unloading the stores, which they managed to accomplish as the enemy anchored off Tarrytown and began a heavy cannonade, under cover of which they sent two gunboats, and four barges to destroy the vessels. Captain George Hurlbert of the Second Dragoons remained on board the most distant sloop from the shore with twelve Second Dragoons to hold off the approaching enemy and defend the American sloops from capture and destruction. Though armed only with their pistols and sabres, Hurlbert kept the pistols concealed until the enemy were alongside, and then gave them a withering fire. The British recoiled, but came on and with sheer weight of numbers managed to board the sloop. Captain Hurlbert finding his detachment surrounded, ordered his Dragoons to jump overboard and make for the shore. Hurlbert, not unlike a real Captain of a ship, remained to the last, then leaped over the rail and safely made the shore with all but one of his Dragoons who had been killed in the desperate fight on the deck. Colonel Sheldon had been effectively covering their swim ashore and now that his Dragoons were off of the American sloop, the same carbine-fire raked the deck of the sloop which the enemy were burning. The carbine fire of Sheldon's Dragoons was too deadly to allow the British to set fire to the other sloop, and they hurriedly retired to their ships.

Captain Hurlbert, Captain-Lieutenant Miles and Quartermaster Shaylor and several Dragoons jumped into the water and made for the sloop, in order to extinguish the fire, which they managed to accomplish in time and saved the vessel. While swimming in the water, Captain Hurlbert received a musket ball through his thigh from one of the retiring British barges. A wound which he was to die from two years later.

About daylight, the American General Howe arrived with a division of troops and Artillery and a battery was opened on the British ships, which obliged them to slip their cables and fall back down the river.

Washing in General Orders of 19 July 1781 praised the Second Dragoon Regiment for their gallant behaviour:

"The gallant behavior and spirited exertions of Colonel Sheldon and Captain Hurlbert of the Second Regiment of Dragoons; Captain-Lieutenant Miles of the Artillery, and Lieutenant Shaylor of the Fourth Connecticut Regiment, previous to the arrival of the troops, in extinguishing the flames of the vessels which had been set on fire by the enemy, and preserving the whole of the ordnance and stores from destruction, entitle them to the most distinguished notice and applause of their General."

Twenty five of Sheldon's Dragoons were assigned to another grand monouvre on 21 July that advanced on the North River Road which gave them a close view of the enemy lines but not much else.

Washington now abandoned any further attempts on New York and marched to Yorktown, Virginia with the American and French armies. The services of Sheldon's Second Dragoons were needed to continue as "The Watchdogs of the Highlands". They could not be spared from this vital role to join the glories of the Yorktown campaign.

Consequently, Heath's Highlands army was greatly weakened by Washington's march to the south. The duty of the Second Dragoons became doubly rigorous. In his orders to General Heath before he left, Washington includes the disposition of Sheldon's Horse:

"Although your general rule of conduct will be to act on the defensive only, yet it is not meant to prohibit you from striking a blow on the enemy's posts or detatchments, should a fair opportunity present itself. Waterbury's Brigade, which may be posted towards the South, Sheldon's Corps, the State troops of New York, and other light parties may occasionally be made use of to hold the enemy in check, and carry on the petit-guerre with them."

The Second Continental Dragoons were not long in fulfilling these orders to the utmost.

While Colonel Sheldon with the bulk of the Regiment remained centralized in the Westchester region, Major Tallmadge and his squadron had a roving commission from General Washington to harass the enemy wherever they could be found.

At Treadwell's Neck, near Smithtown on Long Island, a party of Loyalist wood-cutters, 150 in number, erected a stockade which they called Fort Slongo. This, Major Tallmadge determined to destroy. Moving his squadron into the neighborhood of Norwalk, Connecticut, at the same time he ordered a number of whaleboats to be collected at the mouth of the Saugatuck River. At nine o'clock on the night of 2 October, 1781, Tallmadge embarked 150 of his squadron under Major Lemuel Trescott of the Ninth Massachusetts. They landed at four o'clock the next morning, and at dawn attacked the Fort. Fort Slongo was carried by storm and the garrisson yielded with the loss of only one Second Dragoon wounded. Two of the enemy were killed and as many wounded in the assault. The Dragoons destroyed the blockhouse and two iron four-pounders, made 21 prisoners, including two Captains and one Lieutenant. Embarking safely in their whaleboats the commando Dragoons returned to Connecticut with a brass three pounder, the colors of the Fort, seventy stand of arms, and a quantity of ammunition.

This was a brilliant commando strike. The psychological effect of carrying the war to the enemy's back door was great. The capricious Long Island Sound was no barrier to the many crossings of the Second Dragoon "Marines". Their raids were earning them the publicity of the British Tarleton, without his stigma of cruelty.

Washington thanked Trescott and the whole detachment profusely when he heard of the affair. Sergeant Churchill who had accompanied Major Tallmadge the year before the Fort St. George expedition, behaved so gallantly in leading the advance of the storming party on Fort Slongo that Washington rewarded him with the Badge of Military Merit (Washington had just established honorary badges of distinction in August, 1781. They were to be conferred upon non-commissioned officers and soldiers who had served three years with bravery, fidelity, and good conduct, and upon every one who should perform any singularly meritorious action. The badge entitled the recipient "to pass and repass all guards and military posts as fully and amply as any commissioned officer whatever". A board of officers for making such awards was established, and upon their recommendation the Commander-in-Chief presented the badge.) Dragoon Sergeant Churchill was one of the first Americans to receive the award.

Soon after this exploit, Tallmadge's squadron returned to their old on the lines about White Plains, where with the rest of the Regiment under Sheldon, they had their hands full the remainder of the year in protecting the inhabitants against the marauding encroachments of the Loyalist Corps in Westchester and especially the maraudings of the inevitable Cow-Boys and Skinners.

Some hard cash was brought over from France to Boston in October by Colonel Laurens. A detachment of forty Second Dragoons were sent to escort it to the Continental Congress at Philadelphia. Since this was the first "real" money that the United States had seen for many a moon, a whole Regiment was thrown between the Second Dragoon escort and Westchester, to form a protective screen against the marauding bands of the enemy.

Before the year closed the allied armies under the victorious Washington, returned from the capture of Lord Cornwallis and his British army at Yorktown, and once more took up their quarters on both sides of the Hudson. The winter was spent by Sheldon's Second Dragoons in Connecticut as usual.

CAMPAIGN OF 1782

The spring of 82' saw the Second Dragoons back in their old stamping grounds on the Westchester front.

Major Tallmadge was again detached with his squadron and posted near Long Island Sound. From here they occasionally made incursions to Horseneck and the plains on the lines of the county of West Chester to intercept and prevent the driving of cattle to the enemy in New York. This necessary task fulfilled most of their time, as Carleton, in command of the British at New York, pursued a more peaceful policy and kept close within his lines after the surrender of Cornwallis at Yorktown. This presented few opportunities for the Second Dragoons to reach them in combat.

However, towards the close of the year's campaign, an opportunity presented itself, when 600 British troops came down Long Island into Suffolk county and encamped at Huntington, as if for winter quarters. As soon as Major Tallmadge's espionage forwarded the information to him that a considerable portion of the British Light Horse, including the crack 17th Light Dragoons, covered by a body of infantry, had taken up their quarters at Huntington, on the north side of Long Island, Tallmadge conceived the audacious plan of beating up their seemingly safe quarters.

It was around the close of November, when the enemy on Long Island were relaxed and felt safe from any of Tallmadge's commando raids for the Connecticut side of the Sound. Tallmadge, his plan in readiness, went personally to headquarters and disclosed it to General Washington and requested his permission to execute his raid. Washington nodded in satisfaction, and well aware of Tallmadge's past successes, readily consented and told Tallmadge that he might collect his whaleboats, but not to undertake the endeavor until he named the exact time. The order finally came, the night of the attack was for December 5, 1782. Washington had planned an expedition down the North River at the same time and Colonel Sheldon, with the other squadron of the Second Dragoons, was to have a part in it. Washington's plan was to hurl a large force of his army below Fort Knyphausen, while he moved down with the main body to Fort Independence and King's Bridge. At the same time

Tallmadge would be invading Long Island. The enemy, thus placed between three fires, might have been forced to yield.

Tallmadge's detachment consisted of his squadron of Second Dragoons. Serving dismounted in the whaleboats, they hoped to be able to secure the horses of the British 17th Light Dragoons. Also in Tallmadge's command were four companies of chosen Light Infantry and a body of Connecticut Militia, amounting in all to about 700 men. Avoiding alerting British intelligence, the different detachments of Tallmadge's force met for the first time on the evening of 5 December in the vicinity of Stamford, Connecticut. From there they moved on to Shippan Point where Tallmadge had ordered the boats to assemble. Here, finding such obvious preparations, the officers suspected that a commando endeavor was in the offing. Unfortunately, one of Long Island's capricious storms blew up at sunset as the men were filling their whaleboats. The embarkation was delayed as heavy winds, rain and even a first snow started pelting them. Quickly turning the whaleboats over, the men crawled under them for the night. The next morning the rain and snow had abated, but the Sound was a perfect foam of water thwarting any launching of boats. The second night was spent in the same manner as the first, the men under the overturned whaleboats. The following day word was received that three boats of the enemy from Long Island had taken refuge on one of the Norwalk Islands, a few miles to the eastward of them, windbound like themselves, and could not return to Long Island.

The wind and sea lost some of its violence, and the enemies' three boats appeared on the Sound returning to Long Island. Major Tallmadge ordered six of his best boats, with sails, to be manned with Dragoons, and Captain Brewster, an experienced sailor, was put in command and ordered to overtake the enemy if at all possible. The boats put off from the Connecticut shore, and although their course was before the wind, three of them were obliged to turn back. The enemy, sighting Tallmadge's three boats bearing down upon them, pressed all sail as well as oars, and steered for Long Island.

Captain Brewster steered his course well, and before the enemy had reached the middle of the Sound, which at this point was about twelve miles wide, he fell in with two of their heaviest boats, which they engaged with spirit. On the first fire, every man in one of the enemies' boats fell, either killed or wounded. Captain Brewster received a ball in his chest but the fight was continued and his party captured two of the enemy boats and their surviving occupants, the third and lighter boat managed to escape. For the first time the Second Dragoons had turned sailor and carried off a victorious "naval coup" on the water, thus showing their versatility and ability to win victories, either as cavalry ashore, or on the water.

On the third night a last attempt was made to cross the Sound. The prospects were similarly inviting when the sun set, but as soon as the first boats were in the water the wind came up in gale force and Tallmadge was forced to abandon the enterprise. It undoubtedly was for the best, as the enemy boat that escaped from Captain Brewster must have given the alarm on Long Island.

Washington's part of the attack had also failed as the enemy were warned and sent frigates above Fort Washington (Knyphausen), so that no boats could pass by them undiscovered. It was discovered later that when these attempts were to have been made, the preliminary articles of peace had been actually signed.

As the campaign closed, Colonel Sheldon retired to Connecticut with his squadron for winter quarters, while Major Tallmadge and his squadron remained on Long Island Sound to harass the enemies' shipping throughout the winter.

CAMPAIGN OF 1783

Probably no unit of the Continental army saw as much active service during the closing days of the war as Major Tallmadge's squadron of the Second Continental Light Dragoons.

Through his effective intelligence service, Major Tallmadge was well informed in regard to the smuggling trade that was carried on with the British on Long Island and many of these trading boats fell into his Dragoons' hands.

In the course of the winter Tallmadge was informed that one of the American public armed vessels, or privateer, which was appointed to cruise in the Sound to protect the American commerce and to prevent the smuggling or so called "London Trade", was actually engaged in carrying it on. She was a large sloop called the *Shuldham,* armed and equipped and commanded by Captain Hoyt. Having a minute invoice of her cargo, Major Tallmadge boarded her with a few Dragoons when she docked at Norwalk. Confronting the Captain, he flew into a rage and weighing anchor he put out for Long Island with Tallmadge aboard in spite of Tallmadge's threats. He kept his course heading directly for the enemy fleet at Lloyd's Neck. Finally, when they were almost across the Sound, Captain Hoyt weakened and ordered his crew to put about for Norwalk Harbour. The Captain went ashore and was never seen again, while Tallmadge climbed below and found the London Cargo which he had labeled and condemned.

On 20 January 1783, several more foreign and domestic boats were captured by the Second Dragoon "Marines".

Noticing that one of the enemies' armed vessels frequently passed back and forth from Stratford Point to Long Island, Tallmadge learned that her business was to bring goods over and take produce back in return for the British, as well as to annoy the American commerce through the Sound. Major Tallmadge determined to capture or destroy this menace. Riding over the Bridgeport to find a suitable vessel for his plan, Tallmadge met Captain Hubbel who had just the schooner he needed. Hubbel had been forced to forego his trading because of the menace of the enemy schooner and he was anxious to clear the Sound of its presence. A bargain was soon struck whereby Captain Amos Hubbel would navigate his ship to attack the British schooner and would be compensated for his ship, if unfortunately it should fall into the enemies' hands.

Lieutenants Aaron Rhea and Stanley were held in readiness with 45 Second Dragoons, together with Captain Brewster and his boats' crew of Continental troops, all under the command of Brewster. On the 20th of February, 1783, the schooner was seen close to Stratford Point. The American troops were immediately embarked, with orders not to appear on deck until they were ordered. Captain Hubbel weighed anchor at two PM and two hours later the two vessels were engaged. Hubbel's schooner received the first broadside which crippled the hull, mast and rigging considerably. He managed however, to bring his bow directly across the side of the

British ship. When within a few yards of each other, the order was given for the Dragoons to appear on deck, at the same time Hubbel delivered his broadside and the two ships came in contact. The Second Dragoons poured over the side of the British ship with fixed bayonets and she was captured without the loss of an American. A large part of the British crew were killed and wounded by Hubbel's broadside at such close quarters.

In a few hours both ships were snugly moored at Blackrock Harbour. Tallmadge reported his success to General Washington, who returned his congratulations in a letter dated 26 February, 1783. He gave an order of condemnation of the prize. The ship and cargo were sold and the Second Dragoons and other Americans engaged received the prize money.

This *naval victory* was the last recorded action of the Second Dragoons. On the 18th of April, 1783, Washington ordered the cessation of hostilities, as the preliminary articles of peace had been received by Congress. However, it was by no means certain that peace would follow, and Washington ordered Major Tallmadge to maintain his "secret road" of espionage into New York to keep on obtaining information as to the probable movements of the British.

Two months later however, peace was of such a certainty that the Second Continental Light Dragoons were disbanded on 13 June 1783.

So came to an end this gallant New England corps, after an eight year existence, in which time it had seen continual action and became famous for its daring exploits, while mounted, afoot, afloat, and even "undercover". None of the other three Continental Light Dragoon Regiments could claim such distinctive versatility.

Officer   Trooper   Trumpeter

Plate No. 16

Part Three
BAYLOR'S VIRGINIA-CAROLINA HORSE

THE THIRD CONTINENTAL LIGHT DRAGOONS

    Though Baylor's Horse shared with the First Dragoons the laurels of the victors of the Battle of Cowpens, still they were repeatedly associated with disaster prior to this crowning victory over Tarleton. Of Washington's four Light Dragoon regiments, the Third would undoubtedly epitomize the term *disaster prone.*

63

Lieutenant Colonel George Baylor from Virginia did not gain his regiment of horse entirely from his friendship with George Washington. He had been the Commander in Chief's first aide de camp in the harrowing marginal campaigns of 75' and 76'. Serving with distinction at Trenton and Princeton, Washington chose Baylor to bear the glad tidings of his victory at Trenton and the captured Hessian standards to the President of the Continental Congress then sitting at Baltimore. The favorable comment from Washington of Baylor's part in the victory prompted Congress, as a token of their appreciation of his services as well as the cheering report he had brought on January 1, 1777, to present Baylor with a horse, properly caparisoned. When Washington, at the same time, recommended Baylor for the command of one of the proposed regiments of horse, Congress readily agreed and commissioned him on January 9, 1777, Colonel of the Third Regiment of Continental Light Dragoons. The regiment to be raised primarily in Virginia and possibly North Carolina if necessary.

The other three Dragoon regiments had a head start in their formation and Baylor was ordered by Washington not to waste any time in getting his Dragoons raised, equipped and ready to take to the field.

Although Baylor was to nominate all of his officers except the field officers, who were appointed by Washington, still the customary nepotism, a sign of the times in all armies, prevailed when Washington requested Baylor to appoint two namesakes of his, sons to Lawrence Washington and Robert Washington, as Cornets if the quota of Cornets were not already filled. He also asked Baylor to save a Lieutenantcy in some troop for little William Starke, who was then a Lieutenant in the 6th Virginia Foot.

Baylor had only to raise five troops as the troop of George Lewis, which already existed as Washington's Bodyguard, was to be annexed to the Third Dragoons. The pattern of raising the Regiment was the same as for the other Dragoon regiments. As soon as Baylor had chosen his Captains and Lieutenants, they were dispatched to Virginia and North Carolina to recruit men for Dragoons.

The Third Dragoons missed the preliminary skirmishes at Woodbridge and Short Hills before Howe sailed for Philadelphia. Baylor was having trouble in Virginia in finding men and horses and he could only forward one fully equipped troop, which arrived at Washington's Middlebrook headquarters on June 16, 1777. Washington did not move them up to the front until after the skirmishes.

In August, when Washington's army was near Philadelphia, the Third Dragoons were still not completed. In the middle of August, eighty Militia Dragoons with officers sufficient for three troops of horse arrived in Philadelphia with Brigadier Francis Nash's North Carolina brigade. The horses had been sold as unfit. Since Nash's men had from 12 to 18 months still to serve, an agreement was reached whereby Nash's officers and the Third Dragoon officers were to command the troops in rotation and they were annexed to fill up Baylor's Regiment. They remained as part of the Third Light Dragoons for the remainder of the 77' campaign.

CAMPAIGN OF 1777

Puritanism of the times, or the hypocrisy of it, by today's standards, was apparent in the Third Dragoons. The Regiment had a Chaplain. His qualifying references were his "good character and compelling conversation . . .". His primary purpose was to keep the men from gambling and get them to church on Sundays. If the men were in the field and there were no churches he must be able to make them listen to his lectures or sermons. He apparently did not entirely qualify, as Cornet Baylor, kin to the Colonel, was arrested for gambling.

Efforts were made to eliminate nepotism in the system of officers' promotions. A regimental promotion would automatically be made upon the resignation or death of an officer, by the next officer under him to succeed him. Washington expanded the system by promoting, or exchanging the Dragoon officers, particularly the field officers, from one Dragoon Regiment to another. His uncanny ability to place the right field officer in a particular sphere of operation was invariably for the betterment of that Dragoon Regiment.

As late as August, Baylor was writing Wasington from Virginia that he was having better luck from his officers who were recruiting in West Virginia. The anxious Washington ordered Colonel Baylor to come on with such men as he had ready and to leave officers to recruit for the troops that were deficient. So stood the prognosis of the physical strength of the Third Dragoons for the balance of the campaign of 1777. Their movements within Washington's manouveres in New Jersey and Pennsylvania compared favourably with the other three Dragoon regiments, with occasional variations and exploits of their own.

After Germantown, and the relinquishing of Philadelphia to Howe and the British, since it was increasingly obvious that the horse breeders and farmers were not at all receptive to selling their horses for the Continental dollar, Washington gave his Dragoon regiments the go ahead to impress horses from Loyalists in the area to "horse" the Dragoons without horses. A drastic measure, which gave Washington qualms of conscience. Apparently, he had every intention of repaying the Loyalists for the horses and he set up a formula for identification of the horses. All impressed horses were brought to the Quartermaster General to have the Continental brand put on them and he was to be given the names of the Loyalists from whom they were taken. Unfortunately, several of the more interprising Dragoons, who lacked Washington's honesty and fairness to the enemy Loyalists, abused this order and sold the horses for their own profit. Washington finally had to issue an edict that any Dragoon found without the Continental brand on his horse was to be courtmartialed.

December 5th, saw Washington drawing up his new line of battle for the American army. Bland's and Baylor's 1st and 3rd Light Dragoons were on the right wing and ordered by small detachments to watch the movements of the enemy and to give intelligence of them to see that they did not gain the armies flanks. Thus the Third Dragoons were deployed until the 19th of December, when Washington's army moved up the Schuykill, to Valley Forge, where they entrenched for the winter. The fruitless 77' campaign was over.

CAMPAIGN OF 1778

After experiencing a few weeks of the terribly cold winter at Valley Forge the majority of the Third Dragoons were relieved that their enlistments were up. The Regiment was now considerably reduced in both men, horses and equipment. Captain Cadwallader Jones' Troop was the only one of the Third to be fully enlisted and equipped. However, they were partially "afoot", as they were unable to procure anymore Loyalist's horses and the American farmers would not part with theirs at the limited price (now 120 Continental dollars). Fortunately, several horses that were purchased for the North Carolina draftees to the Third Dragoons were given to Jones' troop as the draftees did not have sufficient horse equipment to stay mounted.

The ever present problem of fodder for the existing horses became so pressing, that it was finally decided to have the Dragoon regiments (including the Third) cantoned in the vicinity of Princeton, New Jersey, for the balance of the winter, where forage was more readily obtainable for the horses. Here they remained until Washington's army took to the field again in the spring.

To compete with the continually rising prices of the inferior quality of the American made cavalry uniforms, arms and horse furniture, both Washington and the "Horse Committee of the Continental Congress" lobbyed strongly for French imports. Washington finally proposed a realistic number of 1500 sets. His proposal stated that the articles would be less expensive and of better quality. They could be smuggled into America in small amounts and thus minimize a disastrous total loss by one sole ship being captured or sunk by the British Navy.

To determine which Dragoon regiment troop was in the most need: A quartermaster (since June 22, 1777) for each troop (in addition to the already authorized regimental quartermaster) was added due to the constant deployment of the individual troops of Dragoons. While Dragoon equipment was a constant task of the troop quartermasters, still, the obtainment of the daily supply of horse forage (fodder) was their prime task. Horse forage was so important throughout the war, that Washington turned down Pulaski's logical requests to set up a central Dragoon horse forage

67

dump close to Trenton, New Jersey, as he feared it would be a prime military objective to the enemy, who were equally in constant need of horse forage.

To re-emphasize: The Continental Light Dragoons were constantly quartered in respect to the horse fodder supply rather than their tactical importance. A very important factor. For this constant prime consideration greatly minimized their strategic value.

The Third Dragoons made their first recorded successful cavalry charge under their Major, Alexander Clough. On May 4, he was sent with a party of the Third to Cooper's Ferry near Bordentown, where 600 British, the 63rd and 55th Regiments, were stationed as guards to a fatigue party of 200 men, who were cutting wood and hunting for forage for the British cavalry in Philadelphia. The fatigue was daily relieved and their lines were covered by three small redoubts without cannon. Clough reconnoitered their picket which was strongly posted. He finally sent two troopers within sight of their lines as a decoy. The ruse was successful as a strong squad of the 17th Light Dragoons galloped out. Major Clough's trumpeter blew the charge and unsheathing their sabres his troop charged upon them. The melee was severe for several moments until the 17th were finally dispersed, after losing four troopers taken by the Third Dragoons. Clough's daring coup was all the more meaningful, as it occurred within sight of the 600 British picket. More important, the four captured horses were in excellent condition and fit for remounts. Major Clough was given $510 for them, or $170 a horse, which was distributed as "prize money" among his Dragoons who took part in the action.

The Third Dragoons were not always as successful. It was imperative to keep the roads patrolled as the British were constantly attempting to make incursions. A junior Lieutenant, John Hill Carter, of Baylor's Horse, was tried at a General Court Martial for neglect in leaving the different roads unguarded from Barren Hill Church to Philadelphia, enabling the enemy to march a body of horse and foot to the church and surprise and make prisoners a subaltern and his Dragoon party, who had returned to the church for refreshment. He was found guilty, but Wasington, upon investigating the matter found that Lieutenant Carter had misunderstood the orders of his senior officer, Captain McLane, and let him off after a reprimandation.

The acute problem of re-supply and remounts was partially solved when Washington resolved that the necessities for each individual regiment of Dragoons would be drawn from the regiment's origin. As Bland's 1st, and Baylor's 3rd Dragoons were both from Virginia, the state was divided between them. So that there would be no conflict and competition for the necessities, the area of procurement for Baylor's Dragoons was the area north of the James River to the Susquehannah, including Maryland (where they were obtaining some recruits) and a portion of Virginia. The 1st Dragoons supply region was south of the James River. By this method of apportionment, the Dragoon Colonels and their troop supply officers would be familiar with their regional manufacturers and the quality, or lack of it, of cavalry necessities, not to mention the best areas for remounts.

Colonel Baylor followed Bland to Virginia, gathering a total of $100,000 in warrants from Congress, Virginia and North Carolina, to re-equipe the 1st and 3rd Dragoons. Washington's logistical regional strategy was apparently successful, for Baylor, on May 11, forwarded 40 men and 50 horses to Washington's camp.

The Third Dragoons were now in a more corpulent state when Clinton, now in command at Philadelphia, marched the British army towards New York. In his meeting and battle with Washington at Monmouth, the Third were actively engaged, but not as a decisive force. After the American victory, they harassed the retreating British army all the way to Sandy Hook, before the British were ferried over to safety in New York City.

The campaign now settled into a status quo with Clinton safe in New York and Washington's army encamped again at Middlebrook (near Boundbrook) in New Jersey. Lieutenant Colonel Byrd (Bird), who commanded the Third in Baylor's absence to recruit and re-supply his regiment, in July was also recruiting, and Major Clough, the hero of Cooper's Ferry, took command until Colonel Baylor returned in August.

By September 22, the Third Dragoons boasted 159 rank and file, with the promise of 20 or 30 more recruits enroute from Virginia.

There now occurred the first of a series of disasters that almost anihilated the Third Dragoons. Colonel Baylor, with 103 of his Third Dragoons were moved up in September and stationed in the vulnerable northeast corner of New Jersey near Old Tappan (exactly 2½ miles SW on Rivervale Road at the Hackensack River, between the Old Tappan Road and Prospect and Washington Aves).

To escape being under the debilitating command of General Wind with his Militia at Old Tappan, Colonel Baylor had posted himself with his Third Dragoons in three barns two and one half miles away. Though General Mad Anthony Wayne commanded the whole, still Wind and Baylor were actually left to their individual resources. Cornwallis was before them at a distance. The British had pushed two bodies of troops across the Hudson on a grand forage into Bergen county, New Jersey, under Knyphausen to the north from King's Bridge and Cornwallis directly in the Tappan area. Baylor was well aware of the movement and, on 22 September, had made a close reconnaissance in person with one of his Dragoon patrols on the Hackensack. Cornwallis was also aware of Baylor's and Wind's positions thanks to his Loyalist informants in the area.

Unaware of any impending disaster, Baylor and his Dragoons were undoubtedly less vigil on the day before their tragedy, for they had just received the very same day, September 27, 200 new uniforms as described below:

CAPS—Polished black leather with red brown horse hair crest and red turban.

HAIR—Natural for active service. Powdered white for dress.

NECK STOCK—Black.

COAT—White, faced with medium blue collar, lapels, cuff and coat tail turnbacks. Silver buttons. Trumpeters may have followed contemporary custom and dressed in reverse facings, viz., a medium-blue coat with white collar, lapels, cuffs and coat-tail turnbacks.

VEST—Medium blue.

BREECHES—White.

BOOTS—Polished black with silver spurs.

SABER AND BELT—Silver hilt with white sword knot (officers' - silver). Black leather scabbard tipped silver, held by a white leather belt over the right shoulder.

70

Derek FitzJames/70

A Private of Baylor's Third
    Continental Dragoons, 1779

Facsimile of a pewter button from the uniform of the
Third Continental Light Dragoons.

TROOPER'S EQUIPMENT—Black leather ammunition waist pouch. A white carbine sling over the left shoulder with silver hook to support the carbine. Carbine and pistol: wooden parts red-brown, metal parts: silver color except brass butt plate, trigger guard, ramrod guides and end stock cap.

OFFICER'S EQUIPMENT—A crimson waist sash and silver colored epaulets. Field officers: epaulets on both shoulders. Captain: right shoulder only. Subalterns (Lieutenants and Cornets): left shoulder only.

TRUMPETER'S EQUIPMENT—A brass trumpet with medium blue and white twisted cording and tassels carried over the left shoulder. Silver epaulets on both shoulders.

HORSE EQUIPMENT—Blue-grey saddle cloth. black holsters covered with black bear fur. Saddle: red-brown or black. Girth: blue-grey. Harness, reins, headstall, breast strap, tail crupper strap and stirrup straps: black. Stirrups and bits: silver. Picket-rein from bridle: white.

HORSE COLORING—Red-brown or darker. Trumpeters rode white or light greys.

Colonel Baylor was justly proud of the crack appearance of his Regiment. The final acquisition of the much sought regimentals had been the result of much "campaigning" by the Third Dragoons procurement officers as well as Washington's intervention. They were finally able to campaign as a unified appearing corps. Unfortunately, their exultation was short lived, for they were on stage that very night in the most tragic performance of their lives.

Determined to cut them off in their exposed position, Cornwallis dispatched a crack commando force under the infamous butcher, Brigadier Grey, consisting of the 2nd Light Infantry, the second battalion of Grenadiers and the 33rd and 64th regiments, from the New Bridge, at nine in the evening. Another party also crossed the Hackensack to cut off Wind's American Militia, but were unsuccessful, the Militia having received warning in time from a British deserter, and Wind changed his position, but without warning Colonel Baylor, which might have prevented the impending disaster.

About two AM of 27 September, Grey's commandos guided by the neighborhood Loyalists, successfully surprised a Sergeant's guard of about a dozen Third Dragoons stationed at a bridge over the Hackensack behind Baylor's camp. After butchering the Dragoon Guard in cold blood, Grey's men quickly and silently surrounded the barns lodging the Third Dragoons and the houses quartering Baylor and his officers along what was then appropriately called "Overkill Road" (now Rivervale Road). Repeating his orders as at Paoli, Grey ordered his men to remove the flints and withdraw the musket charges, affix bayonets and attack without quarter upon the unsuspecting Dragoons. Of the 104 Third Dragoons and officers, 67 were killed or wounded. Many bayoneted before they could arise from their beds. Naked and unarmed, "begging for compassion, being incapable of resistance," for the most part. One British Captain alone heeded their cries for mercy and spared Captain John Swan and all of his 4th troop and they were carried off prisoners. One barn lodging 16 Dragoons managed to partly arm themselves, discharged ten or twelve pistols and engaged the attackers with their broadswords or sabres. The British overpowered them by sheer numbers and bayonetted nine Dragoons before sparing the seven others. Three Dragoons alone broke free from another barn to escape. Captain Robert Smith was lodged in a house with ten Dragoons. They managed to burst outdoors and offered to surrender if given quarter. Instead, he was called "a damned Rebel" and ordered to be bayonetted. Fortunately, Smith had his Dragoon pistol, which he fired at the British officer, "which opened the way for himself and his companions to escape.", which they did by leaping over a fence and losing themselves in a morass. Another Third Dragoon officer, Lieutenant William Barrett, was the only member of the Regiment who managed to escape on horseback.

The Regiment's tragedy was deepened with the loss of their Colonel. Colonel Baylor and Major Clough with two other officers put up a valiant stand when their house (the Haring House) was burst into. They managed to momentarily break free of their overwhelming attackers by forcing the door to a room with a large Dutch chimney, the only means of escape, which they tried to climb up. They were bayonetted in the attempt. One officer, Captain Fitzhugh, was killed. Colonel Baylor (mortally wounded), Major Clough and the fourth, Lieutenant Robert Randolph was spared to

74

be taken prisoner with the wounded Baylor and Clough.

Fortunately, several badly bayonetted Dragoons, including Lieutenant Morrow, were believed dead by Grey's butchers and left on the scene of slaughter, when they moved on to continue their foray into Rockland county. The same morning after Grey's departure, Captain Robert Smith, now temporarily in command, who had managed to escape, returned with the other escapees he could gather, to carry off their comrades who were still alive. Unfortunately, several of them were so badly bayonetted that they died later.

Although not a complete anihilation of Baylor's Third Dragoons, as some historians would have posterity believe, still the massacre near Old Tappan was a crushing blow. Of Baylor's force there of 104 officers and Dragoons, 67 were killed, wounded, or captured. The courageous Major Clough died of his many wounds as well as Captain Fitzhugh. Colonel Baylor, badly wounded by a shot in his lungs, recovered, and was exchanged much later. Captain John Swan was also captured with his troop as well as Lieutenant Robert Randolph, three Cornets and Surgeon George Evans, which was fortunate for the immediate care of his Colonel, for he managed to save Baylor from dying of his critical wounds.

The intensity of the fury of Grey's men was further revealed when it was reported that they even bayonetted to death seventy horses of the Third Dragoons, which is incredible, horses being such a precious commodity on both sides. It was obvious that there were no British cavalrymen in Grey's force. Captain Smith and his survivors had the gruesome task of burying the butchered Dragoons, which they did in Tanning vats in a mass grave. The site was long marked by a millstone used in the tanning operation. The Continental Congress was outraged when their investigation of Dragoon survivors revealed that at least one Dragoon received 16-bayonet stab wounds and three other Dragoons received 12 each. Grey's atrocity charges were confirmed by present day archaeological exhuming of the Dragoon bodies. Skull fractures, apparently by British musket butts, were found.

Captain Smith's return to the Third Dragoons depot at Middlebrook with the 37 survivors (including the wounded who recovered) was a meloncholy sight. Here, they re-joined the two troops totalling 55, who were fortunate enough to have been able to remain there. The Third Dragoons now had a surviving strength of 92, or three small troops. The Regiment however, was now without a field officer to command it, as Colonel Baylor was a prisoner and Major Clough was dead of his wounds. The Lieutenant Colonel, Benjamin Bird, was recruiting in Virginia and expected to be moved up to command. General Washington though had other plans. He soon made one of his wisest choices of command, much to Bird's chagrin: He transfered his cousin, Major William Washington of the 4th Dragoons to the Third. On November 20, 1778, he was commissioned Lieutenant Colonel of the Third and led them after their assumed ashes at Tappan to such glory in Greene's southern army. The disgruntled Benjamin Bird resigned from the Third on 20 November to make room for William Washington.

Fortunately, active campaigning for the balance of 78' ceased when winter followed not too long after the horror at Tappan. The Regiment went into winter quarter at Fredericktown, Maryland to mend their wounds.

CAMPAIGN OF 1779

George Washington had the utmost faith in the potential ability of his cousin William and he originally intended to send him south with his Third Dragoons to assist General Lincoln in his defense of the south which was being taken over by the British. However, an evaluation of the fitness of the Third Dragoons in May revealed that most of the men's enlistments were up and the remaining effectives were in sore need of remounts. Consequently, their departure was delayed until they could be re-built and re-furbished sufficiently to be sent south. They were stationed in Stirling's division at Trenton while they slowly regained their former *figure*.

Apparently, the Third Dragoons had regained their former *color* by September, for the Count de la Luzerne was commenting on the smart appearance of third picked troopers that Lieutenant Colonel Washington had sent to escort him (along with a troop of Lee's Legion) to the Continental Congress in Philadelphia.

At the same time the Third Dragoons replaced Lee's Legion at

Lieutenant Colonel William Washington
Third Continental Light Dragoons

From the portrait by Charles Willson Peal in
Independence Hall, Philadelphia.

Paramus, New Jersey, until 5 November, when they were ordered by General Washington to join General Maxwell's corps at Westfield, New Jersey, to protect the area from an expected grand forage expedition of the British from Staten Island. The foray was abandoned when the British learned of Maxwell's gathering strength.

The Regiment's great southern adventure began on 19 November, 1779, when they finally were ordered to prepare themselves to march to Charlestown, South Carolina, to join Lincoln's southern army. Captain George Lewis's troop, comprising George Washington's bodyguard alone remained in Washington's northern army. It was from this troop's devoted service to Washington and his family during the war that it, as well as the rest of the Third Dragoon Regiment acquired the name "Lady Washington's Own".

Travelling southward via Philadelphia the Regiment remained there while Lieutenant Colonel Washington harassed the board of war with his requisitions for the cavalry necessities that he needed. It was a cold wintry morning in the end of December before they were ready to march. Although they were unaware of the unexpected warm receptions in the warm embraces they would be exchanging there with the infamous Tarleton.

CAMPAIGN OF 1780

William Washington arrived at Charlestown with his Third Dragoons about the same time that Clinton was disembarking his British troops south of the city with the intention of besieging the city. Against this bustling background of desperate preparations for defense General Lincoln dispatched Washington with his Dragoons to harass the enemy's approach in any way that he saw fit.

Tarleton had just disembarked his British Legion of horse and foot and was marauding the countryside to find horses to mount all of his Dragoons. The first encounter between these two cavalry leaders took place on March 26, at Governor Rutledge's Plantation, between Rantowle's Bridge and Ashley Ferry. Both Washington and Tarleton were reconnoitering with their respective corps when they met within 100 yards of the British flying camp. In the fierce conflict that occurred, Tarleton and his Dragoons were completely dispersed by Washington and his Third Dragoons. Tarleton fled to the British line. Washington pursued but wisely ceased when he observed a superior body of British and German Light Infantry and Grenadiers marching across the field to get in back of him. Among the valuable prisoners taken by the Third Dragoons was Colonel Hamilton of the North Carolina Royalists and British Surgeon, Doctor Smith, besides several others. Tarleton also lost seven killed, while Washington's Third Dragoons suffered only one Dragoon badly wounded.

Washington was off to a running start in the deadly Chess game with Tarleton. His foe was a worthy opponent though and he smarted and waited for a crushing move.

Washington's daring partisan leadership, now so apparent, even conceived and put in motion a plan to capture the British commander, Sir Henry Clinton, himself, when he visited the newly arrived reenforcements from Georgia. He very nearly succeeded.

By now the name William Washington was sticking in Tarleton's craw and he became obsessed with the determination to exterminate him. Clinton was encircling Charleston, but Colonel Washington and his Third Dragoons were encamped at Middleton Place (Plantation) near the head of the Ashley River near Goose Creek. From his new headquarters at the Quarter House, six miles above Charleston, Tarleton, on 5 April, led 550 men in an attempt to surprise Washington at Middleton's. Alerted to his advance, Washington left his campfires burning and slipped away to the 23rd Mile House with his cavalry and set up his new camp. Chagrined at his failure, Tarleton retired, but not before Washington, who had a party of his Third Dragoons trailing close, attacked Tarleton's rear guard taking three prisoners.

Meanwhile, the British under Clinton had almost encircled Charleston and began their first parallel. General Huger had been stationed outside the city at Monck's Corner at the head of the Cooper River with all of the American cavalry, in all about 379 Dragoons. Washington had fallen back from his advanced post at the 23rd Mile House with his Third Dragoons to join Huger.

Tarleton's day of reckoning was at hand. Clinton was anxious to close Huger's life-line to Charleston. Tarleton with his Legion and

Fergurson's Riflemen set out from Tarleton's camp at the Quarter House on 12 April, in advance of two British Regiments. His advance guard captured a Negro messenger bearing a message from Huger's camp to Charleston. He was forced to guide them by unguarded paths which avoided the american cavalry patrols. Tarleton moved forward in silence, and at 3 AM on April 14, he struck the American Dragoons at Monck's Corner. Driving in fiercely, he entered the camp with the fleeing videttes. Although the American Dragoon horses were mostly saddled and Dragoons accoutred for action, Tarleton's surprise attack was complete. Colonel Washington and Major Jameson and many of their Third and First Dragoons fled on foot into the swamps bordering the River, their only avenue of escape. They saved themselves by their knowledge of the country. The loss of all of the American Cavalry at Monck's Corner was considerable: 15 were killed, 17 wounded and about 100 officers, Dragoons from the First and Third Regments (and Pulaski's Hussars) were captured. Most important to Tarleton, was the capture of 83 American Dragoon horses and equipment.

This was a crushing first defeat to the Third Dragoons in the south. Fortunately, the vicinity of Monck's Corner was in the very heart of the high bred horse stock raising country and they were able to remount themselves.

While Washington and Jameson gathered their scattered Third and First Dragoons and withdrew to the north of the Santee for security, they were joined by Lieutenant Colonel Anthony White of the First Dragoons, the senior Dragoon officer now present. White and Washington were brothers in arms, they both having served together in Moylan's 4th Dragoons, White as Lieutenant Colonel and Washington as Major.

The two Colonels, soon proved that there still was plenty of bounce left in the American Dragoons in South Carolina. A head count revealed that they still had 272 men left between the Third and First Regiments present, and 250 were effectives.

Discovering that Cornwallis extended his foraging parties to the southern banks of the Santee on which they were encamped, it was decided to interrupt the collection of his supplies. Colonels White and Washington crossed the Santee at Dupui's Ferry on May 5th. The next morning at Wambaw, Colonel Elias Ball's plantation, near Strawberry, they found an officer and seventeen men from Tarleton's command busy foraging. They captured them all. Sweeping to the south, White and Washington planned to recross the Santee at Lenud's Ferry. Here, Colonel Buford had been posted on the opposite shore to send boats across for them. Unfortunately, the boats were late and American Dragoons, instead of moving to a stronger position, incautiously waited on the southern bank of the Santee for the boats.

Unaware of the American Dragoon raid at Wambaw, Tarleton was sweeping north-westward with 150 Dragoons. Meeting a Loyalist who had witnessed the American coup, he received complete information about White's and Washington's line of march, and probable intent of recrossing the Santee at Lenud's Ferry.

The disaster at Monck's Corner was repeated when Tarleton's forced trot brought him to the Ferry at 3 PM. The American Dragoon vedettes were immediately charged and driven into the main body of First and Third Dragoons standing idly on the shore awaiting Buford's tardy boats. The surprise was complete. Only one officer and seven American Dragoons managed to mount and fight their way through Tarleton's Dragoons and escape on horseback. The rest, who were not killed, wounded, or captured by the suddeness of Tarleton's attack, fled into the swamps and hid, including Colonel White. Those directly at the Ferry and too far from the swamps were forced to escape by swimming across the Santee. Washington and Major Jameson were among them. Others, not as good swimmers, drowned in the river.

The Continental First and Third Dragoons lost heavily in this second disaster. Five officers and 36 Dragoons were killed and wounded. Seven officers and 60 Dragoons were taken prisoners, making a toll (or further reduction) of 108. This second disaster gave to the British uncontrolled possession of all of the country between the Cooper and Santee Rivers and extinguished any hopes of maintaining a life-line for a retreat from Charleston. Lincoln surrendered six days later on 12 May.

The fugitive Dragoons gathered at Buford's camp across the Santee, but the Third and First Dragoons were mere remnants of their former strength. Of the 125 Dragoons who made their way to Buford's camp, scarcely fifty out of the two Regiments were mounted and properly equiped for action. Colonel Washington left immediately for North Carolina with the dismounted Third Dragoons. The remaining mounted Third Dragoons marched with Buford to reenforce Lincoln in Charleston, when they received word of his surrender. Their status now quickly changed to that of the hunted. They turned and started a forced march to Camden.

Arriving at Camden they soon learned that it was no sanctuary of safety, for Cornwallis, anxious to wipe out the last semblance of the Continental army in South Carolina, was relentlously in pursuit. Buford and the detachment of the Third Dragoons in his force of Virginians, still might have evaded them, if it were not for the eagerness of Tarleton, who Cornwallis had sent ahead with 270 mounted men to overtake them.

On May 29, 1780, on a sultry 3 PM, Tarleton overtook them near the settlement of the friendly Waxhaws Indians close to the North and South Carolina border. In the battle and Massacre that followed the horrors of Monck's Corner and Lenud's Ferry were repeated for Buford's Continental Infantry, but fortunately, not to the same degree this time, for the Third Dragoons. A Sergeant and four Third Dragoons were captured at the onset, but the rest escaped with Colonel Buford.

The trio of major defeats by Bloody Tarleton was enough for the Third Dragoons who must now seeth inwardly while they licked their wounds and replenished their strength. After Waxhaws they rejoined Colonel Washington in the eastern part of North Carolina where many of the troopers had originated. The heroic failures of the Charleston campaign behind them, the two Colonels, Washington and White, were faced with the problem of how to maintain their two regiments in the field to be instrumental in their continual defense of the south. The two friends decided that the remnant troopers of the First Dragoons would serve with Washington's Third Dragoons, while Colonel White and the officers of the First would return to Virginia to recruit anew.

Anxious to join General Gates, who was enroute from Virginia for the attack on the British at Camden, Colonel Washington penned him pleas to use his influence to assist him in obtaining the necessary equipment and mounts so that he might be able to retake to the field with him. Gates paid no attention to this proper plea and thus deprived him of these experienced veterans. Gates' short, but disastrous campaign against Camden showed his need for a sufficient body of *experienced* Light Horse. Gates may have been regurgitating on his glorious victory at Saratoga, which had been won with negligible use of cavalry. Here, on the rolling plains of the south, the Light Horse, after Camden played a paramount part in all of the campaigns. The Third Dragoons were not allowed to inagurate their re-birth and southern successes until after the battle of Camden, where their deployment at full strength may have turned the tide in the battle.

The year entered late fall, with the Third Dragoons, now tempered with determination to atone for their humiliation and suffering from Tarleton at Monck's Corner and Lenud's Ferry. As they rebuilt their strength in the comparitive unmolested regions of North Carolina, their wounds healed, but were ever reminiscent reminders of their humiliation. They were soon to emerge from their lair and inagurate such brilliant retalitary strikes that they earned the reputation of the most actively successful Light Dragoon regiment of either the American or British forces.

WINTER CAMPAIGN OF 1780-1781

When Gates was gathering the remains of his American force at Hillsborough, North Carolina in late 1780, after his defeat at Camden, Colonel William Washington joined him there with four small, but completely acoutred and mounted Dragoons (the Third and remnant of the First) numbering eighty men. Sabres had been a difficult item to obtain. Colonel Washington heard through the grapevine that his native Virginia had Dragoon Sabres in the Richmond Arsenal. He immediately dispatched his supernumeracy of Dragoon officers to obtain them. The bulk of the officers to stay in Virginia to recruit, and the others to return with the sabres. When Washington and his Dragoons selected a sabre from the shipment upon their arrival, it was not unlike "Russian Roulette", as many were defective, as Washington himself discovered in a forthcoming hand to hand duel with Tarleton when his sabre shattered near the hilt.

Fortunately for the continuance of American resistance in the South, General Nathaniel Greene had been sent south by General Washington to rally the surviving American remnants after Camden. One of his most talented Brigadier Generals was the veteran rifleman Daniel Morgan. He arrived in Hillsborough and was given the command of the light corps, including the Third Dragoons. The army moved up to Charlotte and Morgan's brigade was dispatched to Hanging Rock to intercept the exodus of the Loyalists to Camden. The Loyalists forewarned, escaped, but it was learned that a considerable body of them were assembling at Rugely's Farm. Colonel Rugeley had made his farm a recruiting headquarters, as he had been promised a Brigadier's commission if he could recruit enough Royalists (Loyalists). However, his farm was only ten miles from the British main army at Camden, too close for an attack by Morgan's slower moving infantry. A possible strike against Rugeley was entrusted to the more mobile Colonel Washington and his Third Dragoons.

The following incredible coup launched Washington and his Third Dragoons upon their ride to glory in the south. They arrived at the farm on 4 December 1780 to find Rugely, warned of their approach, snugly enclosed in a strong log barn, around which, had been constructed an entrenchment and line of abatis, impervious to everything but Artillery. Washington, aware that his meagre squadron was inadequate for an assault, resorted to partisan strategy. He ordered several of his Dragoons to prepare the trunk of a small pine tree into a reasonable facsimile of a cannon. Mounting it upon a nearby farm wagon, he then had them drag the "cannon" to the edge of the clearing and similate an artillery crew about ready to fire their piece. Then Washington, tongue in cheek, sent a Corporal under a flag to the fort summoning Rugeley to an immediate surrender. The gravity with which the farce was enacted confirmed the intended idea on Rugeley, who surrendered, believing he had no option. Rugely marched out without firing a shot with his garrison of 112 men. Besides the prisoners, a large quantity of provisions and forage were collected. After burning the fort, Washington and his Third Dragoons returned in triumph to Morgan. This exploit of Washington definitely *out-generalled* Colonel Rugely, as Cornwallis did not elevate him to Brigadier

84

when he was later paroled.

Greene's meagre American army was resigned to that of a harassing force until their numbers could more equal Cornwallis's army. However, Washington and his Third Dragoons, moved out of Charlotte in Morgan's detached brigade who were to act as a harassing commando force. The Third Dragoons were soon to continue their victorious momentum and atone for Monck's Corner and Lenud's Ferry.

Learning that the Loyalist, Colonel Waters, with 250 Raiders was laying waste American settlements of Fair Forest Creek, Morgan dispatched Colonel Washington on 28 December with his eighty Dragoons and Major McCall and 200 mounted Militia on a forty mile forced march to overtake Waters' Raiders who had retired to Hammond's Store in Laurens County, South Carolina. Here they were surprised at noon on 29 December by Washington and McCall. Waters' Raiders made a run for their horses, but Washington extended his mounted Militia on the wings, at the same time charging them in front with his own Third Dragoons. A massacre ensued particularly by the uncontrollable fury of the Loyalist hating American Militia of Major McCall, notwithstanding the restraining efforts of Colonel Washington.

When the fierce melee ended, 150 Loyalists were killed or wounded and 40 taken prisoners. Colonel Waters escaped with the remaining 60. Washington's force did not lose a man.

Though dangerously advanced within the ring of Cornwallis's forces, Washington could not resist a further strike, against the Loyalist Fort Williams at William's Plantation, close to Fort Ninety Six. He sent Colonel Joseph Hayes with 40 Militia Infantry and Cornet Simmons with a squad of ten Third Dragoons to surprise the garrison. Cornet Simmons and his Dragoons arrived ahead of Hayes and his slower infantry to find Fort Williams' garrison of Brigadier Cunningham and 150 Loyalists preparing to abandon the Fort. Although too many for his meagre squad of ten Dragoons to attack, Simmons decided to emulate a ruse worthy of his Colonel Washington. He hid his ten Dragoons in the woods and boldly advanced with a flag demanding Cunningham's surrender. Believing Washington's whole squadron was surrounding him in the woods, Cunningham begged for a five minute parley with his officers. The news of the massacre at Hammond's Store had preceded Cornet Simmons however, and Cunningham's garrison of Loyalists did not await his decision to surrender. They bolted and ran for the woods but not without some casualties. With some prisoners taken, Simmons found great quantities of grain, forage and provisions. After loading as much as his Dragoons were able to carry off, the remainder were destroyed with the Fort.

Re-joining Washington, the successful commando force was returning to Morgan when they met a reenforcement of 200 Americans sent by the worried Morgan who, upon hearing of their deep penetration within 15 miles of Fort Ninety Four, had dispatched the reenforcement to cover Washington's retreat if necessary. Morgan's fears were ill-founded for Washington's commando expedition arrived wearily but safely and exultant on January 6th.

As a consequence of Washington's expedition, the disafected Loyalists in South Carolina did not rally to the British standard for some time. Washington's raid had penetrated so close to the formidable "96" that Cornwallis firmly believed that Morgan had serious designs against that important post. Not being able to rely on the assistance of Loyalists after their disaster at Hammond's Store, he decided not to await for more reenforcements but sent Tarleton to destroy Morgan, or force him to retreat to the rear, where he would endeavor to cut him off.

The above events were the prologue for the drama of the great American victory at Cowpens and the turning of the tide for American resistance in the south. It was also the start of a series of reknowned American cavalry charges under Colonel Washington in the south that prompted General Greene to later exclaim to George Washington that ". . . the enterprise of his [Washington's Third Dragoons] cavalry was unexcelled in the world.".

Morgan was aware of Cornwallis's nutcracker encirclement plan against him. He quickly abandoned any thoughts against Fort Ninety Six, and retired to the Broad River and moved rapidly up its western branches until he came to the "Cowpens", an enclosure for cattle just south of the North and South Carolina border. Here, safer from Cornwallis encircling his rear (at least momentarily), he determined to make a stand to confront Tarleton on 17 January, who had moved rapidly after him. Both sides with approximately

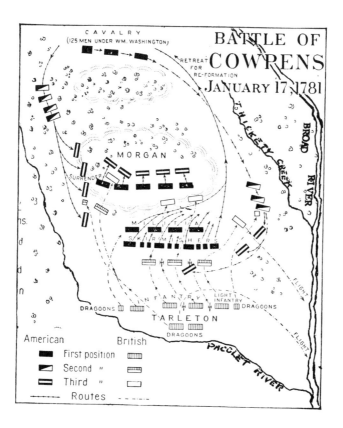

Courtesy, The Pageant of America, by William Wood, New Haven-Yale University Press, 1927 'Winning of Freedom' Volume, map by Gregor Noetzel.

This excellent Cowpens battle map depicts the 3 crucial positions during the battle. Because of their strategic locations the Broad River, Pacolet River, and Thickety Creek have been overlaid. The N. Carolina border was 5 miles directly north where Broad River turned west.

Battle of Cowpens from the original picture by Chappel
depicting the famous Washington-Tarleton duel

1,000 men each were equal in numbers.

In the swale, behind the summit of Cowpens, Colonel Washington was posted in reserve out of sight with his eighty Third (and remnants of the First) Light Dragoons and Lieutenant Colonel James McCall with forty five mounted infantry armed with Dragoon sabres. At the height of the battle, they enacted the decisive turning point against Tarleton's superior force of his Legion Dragoons and 17th British Light Dragoons totalling 250. While his cavalry remained out of sight, Washington had a horseback view of the battle. When Tarleton sent the 17th Light Dragoons to turn Morgan's left flank, Washington's Dragoons erupted upon them as if appearing from the bowels of a volcano and drove them back, then retired as if back into the mountain. When the American Militia infantry retired to re-form as planned, Tarleton threw his complete force into the action, believing the Americans were routed. From his bird's-eye commanding eminence, Washington quickly appraised the situation and sent word to General Morgan: "They're coming on like a mob.' Give them one fire and I'll charge them." Morgan received Washington's message just as his Militia infantry reached their new position. He ordered them to "Face about! Give them one fire, and the day is ours!" Which they did most effectively, and then charged the British with the bayonet. Simultaneously, Washington's Dragoons poured down again to charge among the British infantry. About 200 yards from the battle front they also corralled the leaders and rounded them up like stampeding cattle. The hated Green Dragoons of Tarleton's Legion had no stomach for a determined frontal attack by a foe, especially one that they had surprised and butchered twice over, when they were afoot and helpless. Tarleton's Dragoons, his reserve, refused to respond adequately to Tarleton's desperate command to outflank Morgan's army. Washington fell upon them in their spineless indecision, charging completely through their hated foe in the first charge with terrible effect. Washington quickly wheeled his Dragoons and re-charged on the butchers of their comrades at Monck's Corner and Lenud's Ferry. Though outnumbered two to one, the Third Dragoons took Tarleton's Green Dragoons completely by surprise and a rout ensued.

Recognizing Tarleton himself attempting to re-organize his

routed Dragoons, Washington ordered another charge upon the retreating Green horse, and set off far ahead of his squadron with only his Sergeant-Major and Trumpeter, so eager was Washington to confront Tarleton personally. What followed was probably the most famous hand-to-hand duel of the war. Overtaking Tarleton, Washington encountered first the officer on Tarleton's right, but his slash at him broke his sabre near the hilt. The British officer rose in his stirrups for the coup de grace, but Washington's Bugle boy (Trumpeter) rode past and incapacitated his sword arm with a pistol shot through the British officer's shoulder. At that moment, the officer on Tarleton's left cut at the practically disarmed Washington, but the blow was deflected by Sergeant Major Perry of the Third Dragoons. Tarleton now charged Washington. His enormous well made sabre raised. Washington parried the slash with his broken sabre managing to inflict a lasting wound and crippling of Tarleton's right hand. Reining his horse in a circle, Tarleton snatched out his pistol and fired. The ball barely grazed Washington's knee but wounded his horse. Quickly changing to another horse, Washington ordered his Dragoons, who had now all come up, to follow him in the pursuit of the now fleeing Tarleton and his Green Dragoons.

Washington had every reason to believe that he could overtake Tarleton and capture him with the forty British Dragoons who had rallied around him. Unfortunately, a bend in the road obscured the fleeing Tarleton long enough for Washington to believe that he must have taken the road to the Pacolet River, when actually, Tarleton followed the road to the Broad River. Eventually, realizing his mistake, it was too late to overtake Tarleton, in spite of a twenty mile chase. On their way back to the Cowpens, Washington's Third Dragoons managed to round up 100 more prisoners.

Returning to the battlefield, Washington and the Third Dragoons found that Morgan, in spite of his total defeat of Tarleton, had no illusions as to his exposed position and fully aware that Cornwallis was closing in on him, had retired across the Broad River where Colonel Washington rejoined him that evening.

Tarleton had lost in the one hour fierce battle: 100 killed, 39 of them officers, a consequence of Morgan's definite orders to aim for the epaulettes. He left as prisoners, 229 wounded and 600 prisoners, 27 of them officers, 2 cannon, 800 muskets, 100 Dragoon horses and 35 wagons. Morgan's force had only 12 killed and 60 wounded. For outstanding valour, Colonel Washington was presented with a silver medal and sword (which he sorely needed after his duel with Tarleton) by the grateful Congress. Other Third Dragoons officers who were cited were Captain William Barrett (Va.); Lieutenant Henry Ball (Va.); and Cornet Simmons (S.C.) soon to be promoted to Lieutenant.

The massacres of Monck's Corner and Lenud's Ferry, and even Tappan, were atoned for. Washington and his Third Dragoons complete defeat of Tarleton and his Green Dragoons in a pitched battle had established them as ". . . unexcelled in the world.".

Tarleton (though still active), and his dreaded Legion, who managed to survive, never regained their former stature of respect and terror. No longer was Tarleton the golden boy in Cornwallis's eyes. The British consensus of Tarleton's utter defeat at Cowpens was probably best expressed by one officer: "During the whole period of the war no other action reflected so much dishonour upon the British arms . . .".

While Morgan set an evasive course away from Cornwallis's overwhelming army, Washington and his Third Dragoons were entrusted with getting the British prisoners to the rendezvous on the Catawba River by taking a more northerly route to ensure that the prisoners were not re-taken. A week later Washington made the junction with Morgan on the Catawba.

Cornwallis was close behind. General Greene re-united his small army and continued the retreat northeast to the Dan River, close to reenforcements in Virginia. This began a series of retreats, first by the American, then the British army, which were the most memorable in the annals of war. When Greene's American army finally turned and confronted the British, his army continued their commando tactics of cut-and-run, which saved the south and made General Washington's victorious Yorktown campaign possible.

In the battles of Wetzell's Mill, Guilford, Hobkirk's Hill and Eutaw Springs, Colonel Washington and his Third Dragoons continued their decisive actions that had established their fame at Cowpens, not always winning the battle, but winning the campaign.

At Guilford, in the most critical moment of the battle, in the face of a withering fire, Washington's Third Dragoons charged the regiment of Guards commanded by Colonel Stewart, who fell mortally wounded. A rout followed amongst the Guards and they broke and fled with the Third Dragoons in pursuit. Corporal Francisco, a Virginian of the Third Dragoons, cut down eleven British Guards in succession with his sabre. One of the Guards pinned Francisco's leg to his horse with a bayonet. Refusing to surrender, he assisted the Guard to withdraw his bayonet, then with terrible force brought down his sabre and cleft the poor Guard's head to his shoulders. Colonel Washington seeing an officer surrounded apparently by his staff and supposing it was Lord Cornwallis, he charged forward to take him prisoner. At this moment his Dragoon helmet fell from his head. Washington leaped to the ground to recover it. Following closely behind at the head of the squadron was Captain John Watts (commanding the First Dragoons Company in Washington's squadron) second in command of Washington's squadron. At this critical moment he was shot through the body and became incapable of managing his horse. The animal wheeled and galloped back. Believing that Washington had directed the movement, the Third Dragoon squadron turned and followed. This alone saved the remnant of the British Guards from total destruction by the Third Dragoons. The retreat to the Dan and battle of Guilford were to the American South what the retreat through New Jersey and the battles of Trenton and Princeton were to the North. They turned the tide. Greene lost the battle, but won the campaign.

In the battle of Hobkirk's Hill near Camden on 25 April, the Third Dragoons were hampered by thick underbrush, which brought their flank manouver out of the brush too far behind the battle line. Green's infantry having broke, he ordered a retreat. Washington and his Regiment being over extended, had barely time to retire, which they managed to do after paroling 150 of their 200 prisoners. Mounting the other 50, who were all of the British Surgeons' staff, on the backs of their horses behind his troopers, Washington rejoined Greene's retirement in time to be instrumental in helping Greene save his artillery.

After an abortive attempt to besiege Fort Ninety Six, Greene's army retired momentarily to recuperate and rest in the hills of

The Battle of Hobkirk's Hill

Charge of Colonel Washington's cavalry against the British right flank to cover the American retreat.

Santee, but there was no rest for Washington and the Third Dragoons. They were detached down the country across the Santee to strike all the communications between the enemy and Charleston. On this raid they succeeded in falling in with two parties of the enemy Horse and taking fifty prisoners.

On September 8, the fate of the Third Dragoons came full circle in the culminating battle of Eutaw Springs, not far from the Regiment's massacre site at Monck's Corner. The battle was another tragedy for the regiment, for the thick brush again hampered their charge. Ordered to envelope the British flank, Washington's courageous charge was tragic. Lieutenant Stuart led the first section of Third Dragoons. As they drew near the enemy, they found the ground thickly set with black Jack, which formed almost an impenetrable abatis around the British infantry. The Dragoons were constantly raked by enemy fire no matter which way they swerved. Disaster followed. All but two of the Regiment's Dragoon officers had fallen. Captain John Watts (1st Dragoons), second in command, fell first, pierced by two balls. Then Lieutenants King and Simons suffered similar fates. And worst of all, Washington's horse was shot from under him and he became entangled in the fall. While struggling to free himself, he was bayoneted and a moment more would have received a death thrust when a British officer fortunately interceded, saved his life and made him a prisoner. Lieutenant Stewart's complete troop were either killed or wounded, with Stewart himself severely wounded and his horse killed close to the enemy. The gallant young Carlisle from Alexandria, Virginia, a Cadet in the Regiment, was killed. Half of the Third Continental Light Dragoons were killed or wounded. Finally, Captain William Parsons, who was now in command, assisted by Lieutenant Gordon and Cornet Simmons sounded the retreat and withdrew with the torn fragments of the Regiment. Regrouping, they made still another charge with the American infantry but were again forced to withdraw with Lieutenant Gordon being wounded in the process. Both Americans and British claimed a victory. It was no victory for the Third Dragoons however.

The British retired to Charleston and Greene's army followed and besieged the city until it was evacuated a year later. The Third Dragoons, now led by Captain William Parsons, harassed the

British foraging parties from the city.

In June 1782, the regiments were re-united with their original Colonel. Colonel Baylor, having been exchanged, joined the regiment and on June 13, was given the command of the mounted Dragoons of his Third Light Dragoons and Moylan's 4th mounted Dragoons as well as those of Lee's, as both Moylan and Lee had left the service.

The cavalry had been re-organized in January 1781 and the Light Dragoon regiments were to be on a Legionary corps establishment (horse and foot). This was convenient to the remnants of the Third Dragoons now. They had been so decimated at Eutaw Springs that out of the fifty odd men remaining, about half of them were dismounted. The end of the war was in sight and nothing was being done to put the cavalry back on a respectable footing. The dismounted troop was augmented with the infantry of Lee's Legion, the Delaware Regiment, and one hundred men properly officered and fit for Light Infantry service commanded by Major Beall, and all under the command of Lieutenant Colonel Laurens. Arrangements were made that whenever the Cavalry of any corps were ordered out and infantry was needed, the infantry belonging to such Dragoon Regiment would march with it.

On November 9, 1782, the fragments of the First and Third Continental Light Dragoons were consolidated and thereafter known as Baylor's Dragoons (See Appendice III).

After the British evacuated Charleston on 14 December 1782, Baylor's consolidated Dragoons, 200 strong, actively commanded by Major John Swan, were posted near Combahee to be at hand for the protection of Georgia from the British at St. Augustine, as well as for the convenience of forage. Here they remained until the spring of 1783 until the spread of the peace rumours when the bulk of the mounted Dragoons joined the Sergeant Dangerfield uprising (as related in Part One - The First Continental Light Dragoons).

Their chronicle came to a close when the dismounted Dragoons quartered at James Island, were finally transported back to Virginia. For many of the Third Dragoons it had been a long seemingly exodus from their native Virginia.

The Third Continental Light Dragoons were the most actively reknown of General Washington's four Dragoon Regiments.

Though seemingly disaster prone, they repeatedly rose from their ashes to carry on. Their excellence of officers set the pace for the Regiment. The Third Dragoons officers and mens determination to win out over their numerically superior enemy were classic examples of the best American Patriot.

It may very well be recorded that the fact that the Third Dragoons, under their brilliant William Washington, in the south with Morgan and Greene, played a decisive role in winning the Revolutionary War for the Americans.

Officer   Trumpeter   Trooper

Part Four
MOYLAN'S PENNSYLVANIA HORSE

THE FOURTH CONTINENTAL LIGHT DRAGOONS

The sharp Yankee sense of the true value of the Continental dollar almost prevented the raising of the most worthy little regiment of horse.

First their inception: — On January 8, 1777, General Washington handed Stephen Moylan of Philadelphia a Colonel's commission to raise and command a regiment of Continental Light Dragoons. Moylan had been a most valued member of Washington's staff since August 1775, first, as the Muster-Master-General of the Continental Army; then as Colonel-Quartermaster-General by June, 1776.

From Morristown, Moylan hastened to Philadelphia to raise his regiment. The first stage proceeded smoothly, if not rapidly, for there were many eager aspirants for commissions in the sought after service, in a regiment of horse. The pattern of selection was the same as that in the other three Dragoon regiments. The officers were chosen first from the better established families. George Washington's cousin, William Washington, was given the Major's berth, to later become the most famous Dragoon leader of the war.

A contingent of Moylan's new officers under Major Washington were dispatched to Maryland to recruit troopers, while Colonel Moylan remained in Pennsylvania to do the same. It was now that the true value of the Continental dollar became apparent. With his commission, Moylan had received a $2,000 warrant from the frugal Washington to raise his regiment. Moylan distributed this amongst his new officers, who bought horses for their troopers. Mounts being the obviously most essential piece of equipment for a cavalryman. The farmers and horse breeders had an instinctive distrust of any warrant for the Continental dollar, even from General Washington, and the bargaining was one-sided for the dubious new dollar. Consequently, not near enough horses were acquired with the $2,000 warrant and it was not long before Moylan's officers were pressing him for more money.

His experience as Muster-Master and Quartermaster on Washington's staff had alerted Moylan to Washington's sometimes short-sightedness in Army finance. He now realized that if he was to get his new regiment literally *off the ground* and mounted, he would have to substitute the army warrant for a possibly more acceptable medium of exchange. Moylan wrote Washington suggesting that he draw an order on the Committee of Congress for sufficient funds to complete the raising of his regiment. He emphasised to Washington that it would save the trouble of army warrants and spare his

Colonel Stephen Moylan
Fourth Continental Light Dragoons

Painted after the Revolution. Note the
resemblance to the popular portrait of
George Washington.

Artist unknown

military chest. Washington concurred for on February 26, May 16, and May 30, Congress ordered three warrants issued in favour of Colonel Moylan for $10,000, $10,000 and $25,000.

Moylan was ordered by Congress to lay before the Board of War an account of the expense of raising and equipping a regiment of horse. A difficult order to fulfill, for Moylan soon found that the Continental dollar was no easier to pass, or *horse-trade* with, even though it was backed and authorized by the Continental Congress instead of the Army. The dollar was as unstable and inflationary then as it was almost a bi-centennial later.

It took the sheer patriotism of a few unwise horse dealers to make it possible for Moylan's horse to take to the field. On April 14, 1777, Colonel Moylan was ready for Maryland with his mounted contingent. The rendezvous was to be with Major William Washington there who was finally equally successful in securing mounts.

However, Moylan did not immediately leave Philadelphia for the rendezvous until he had completely armed and trained his raw recruits, the heavy rains notwithstanding. Which was undoubtedly a wise decision as hostile veteran British forces were reported operating in the Delaware bay region. Moylan sent word to Major Washington to do likewise and train and drill his squadron through cavalry manouvers.

The 4th Continental Light Dragoons first baptism to conflict was almost with their own patriot Americans. A quantity of British regimentals (red, intended for the 8th and 21st British foot) had been captured from the enemy. Though wanted by many un-uniformed Continental units in Washington's army, Moylan was able to acquire them for his own Dragoons, red color notwithstanding. The inflamatory hue was almost the undoing of a detachment of the 4th Dragoons who were sent to guard money sent to Washington at Morristown. Thinking they were British 16th Light Dragoons (the uniforms being the same colour, red, faced with blue), the American patriots in the countryside fired upon them. Fortunately, their shots were distant ones and the 4th suffered no casualties.

When the detail arrived at Washington's headquarters and he learned of the near tragedy, he immediately penned Moylan orders to dye the red uniforms, not caring what colour, as long as the

100

present red colour be changed. Until they could be dyed, they were ordered to wear the American hunting frock over the coats when in the field.

Finding green dye the best colour to cover the red, Moylan's Dragoons were soon wearing for the campaign of 1777 the following uniforms:

Green coats trimmed with red cuffs and facings and red waist-coats.

Green cloaks with red capes.

Buckskin breeches and black leather caps trimmed with brown bearskin.

Moylan, now believing his regiment ready to take to the field proceeded with them to Morristown, where he finally joined up with his squadron under Major Wasington. His united 4th Dragoons encamping near the other three Dragoon regiments.

At this time a proposition to commission aGeneral of Horse was considered by Congress. Colonel Moylan, being the senior Light Dragoon Colonel hoped for the Brigadiership. Evidently the commission was to have gone to Thomas Reed however. He had lately been named as a Brigadier General by Congress. Instead, Reed appears to have been made Paymaster-General and the Generalship of the Light Horse was not bestowed on anyone at this time.

CAMPAIGN OF 1777

In May and June, at Washington's new encampment at Middle-brook, the 4th Dragoons acted as Washington's eyes and were posted in front of the American Army covering the region around Middlebrook, Woodbridge and Spanktown, to determine when and where the British fleet were bound for.

The strength of the 4th Dragoons at this time consisted of: Captain Thomas Dorsey's troop at 1 Captain, 1 Lieutenant, 1 Cornet, 1 Quartermaster, 2 Sergeants, 1 Farrier, 2 Wagonners, 40 Rank and File and 6 women, apparently Laundresses, or at least under the guise as such, as was the common practice in all regiments at that time.

Captain David Hopkins' troop of 55.

Captain David Plunkett's troop of 54 at Spanktown.

Captain Charles Craig's troop of over 19.

Handful contingents were also commanded by Captains William Bird, Moore Fauntleroy and Vashel Howard.

Apparently the regiment comprised only four nearly completed troops at this time with a total strength of approximately 180, considerably below their authorized strength.

The variety of the American patriot mind of loyalty and justification of means of correcting errors of omission manifested itself on July 20th. The omission being the fact that the regiment had not been paid for six months as all available funds had been dispensed in acquiring horses, arms and equipment at inflationary prices. At midnight, two Sergeants, two Corporals and fifteen troopers of Captain Charles Craig's Pennsylvania troop deserted and slipped away towards Philadelphia. Moylan, as soon as he learned of the defection, dispatched Lieutenant Colonel White and Major Washington with two troops to overtake them. The chase was long and hard for the deserters outpaced them for forty miles, almost to Philadelphia, before they were finally overtaken and returned to Colonel Moylan, who placed them under guard to await a Court-martial.

The intensity of the pursuit was apparent. Moylan's Dragoons were to have moved to New Windsor, by way of Clone, the same day that the pursued and pursuers returned, but were unable to, because the horses involved in the chase were so stiff that they could scarcely move. However, the next day Moylan's 4th Dragoons broke camp and moved to Bound Brook near New Windsor with the 1st Dragoons.

On July 23, Colonel Moylan personally went to South Amboy to observe the enemy fleet in the lower bay off of New York. He was rewarded by seeing the fleet leave the bay about noon for the open sea. Finally, the British fleet had sailed, where, Moylan did not know. At last he could send the news to General Washington that he had been so long awaiting. This report, with others confirming, led Washington to hasten forward to the southward all of his forces to protect Philadelphia from an attack by Howe.

Moylan's 4th Dragoons were ordered to the vicinity of Philadelphia on July 25, and Moylan to place himself under the commanding officer there. Arriving in haste, by way of Princeton, to cross the Delaware at Trenton, the regiment's baggage and camp women had to follow later.

While the 4th Dragoons encamped outside Philadelphia with the army at the Neshaminy Camp, a Court-Martial was held on August 7, 12, and 16, to try Moylan's deserters. Colonel Sheldon of the 2nd Dragoons presided as the impartial President. Although adjudged *worthy of death*, General Washington pardoned them all, but they were ordered to quit the horse service and enter the foot service "in the corps to which they shall be assigned." Two troopers, apparently the ringleaders, were first found guilty and sentenced to twenty five lashes "on their bare backs". Washington approved of the sentence, but remitted the penalty.

At the same time, Edward Wilcox, Quartermaster to Captain Dorsey's troop, though not a deserter, received a most humiliating sentence for taking a horse and accoutrements belonging to a trooper of his own 4th Dragoons. Found guilty as charged, Wilcox was sentenced to be led around the regiment on horseback with his face towards the tail and his coat turned wrongside outwards and then discharged from the army.

While outside Philadelphia, all leaves and furloughs were forbidden before Washington's army moved back near Germantown on August 8th. Acting as Militiary Police, Moylan was ordered to post his most capable officers with adequate commands of men on all the roads leading from any part of the camp into Philadelphia. Orders were to intercept any Dragoons, or other members of Washington's army who might attempt to slip through for a visit to the city's taverns for tippling or fraternizing with the local doxies. Much to the disgruntlement of the Dragoons, Moylan's cordon of *police* were effective. In fact, the whole body of horse was assigned to bring up the rear of Washington's moving army on the eighth to pick up any stragglers.

At Germantown, Chaplain Samuel Williamson of Moylan's Dragoons gave his intensions to go to Europe to prosecute his studies. Though well liked by the regiment, the Supreme Executive Council of Pennsylvania on August 23, granted him permission, with an excellent recommendation to the Civil and Military officers of the countries to which he might go.

The same day, the 23, news came of the arrival of the British fleet in the Chesapeake, whereupon the 4th Dragoons and Washington's army started southward to meet the enemy.

Breaking camp on Sunday, August 24, they started at four AM to march through Philadelphia. Washington's motive was to stir the martial and patriotic sentiments of the men in the city with the hope of obtaining recruits.

The Light Horse, or Continental Dragoons, moved in two wings. The 1st and 3rd regiments on the right and the 2nd and Moylan's 4th on the left, 150 yards in the rear of General Maxwell's Brigade. Washington was very explicit in ordering that no women belonging to the army were to be seen with the troops in the parade march through Philadelphia.

The next day, on the 25, the American army of ten thousand, crossed the Schuylkill River at the Market St. Ferry and that evening encamped at Darby. Wilmington, Delaware was reached the following day. Here, Washington, taking Moylan and his 4th Dragoons and the 1st and 3rd Dragoons, reconnoitered the country and learned that the British had landed at the Head of Elk River, Maryland, on the day before.

On September 3, Moylan's Horse made the initial encounter of the opposing armies and also the first action of the 4th Dragoons. A strong column under Cornwallis and Knyphausen made a feint of attacking the American front with menacing manouvering, but with the appearance of the 4th and 2nd Continental Dragoons, they retired. Having no mounted cavalry of their own, their own 16th and 17th Light Dragoons were afoot, their horses having died aboard ship enroute from New York to the Chesapeake.

This incident alone should have awakened General Washington to the advantages of employing his Continental Light Dragoons as a massed body against the British. With the British Light Dragoons afoot, Washington's own four regiments of horse, though numbering less than five hundred collectively, could have raised havoc with Howe's army. The Continental Dragoons, posted en-body, on Washington's right, would have prevented Howe's surprise crossing of the Brandywine and his turning of Washington's flank there at the forthcoming Battle of Brandywine. Washington's forced retirement up the Schuylkill and Howe's eventual unopposed occupation of Philadelphia might have been prevented. William Washington, present Major of the 4th Dragoons, later proved the indispensability of charging American Continental Dragoons at the Battle of Cowpens and with far less Dragoons involved. Washington *crossed his Rubicon* when he did not commit his Dragoons at Brandywine. Instead, he employed the Dragoons primarily for orderly duty. Washington even failed to send the Dragoons on vital patrols to ascertain Howe's surprise manouvers during the battle. Only part of Moylan's 4th were in frontal action at Brandywine. Captain Charles Craig's troop were actively engaged. Captain Craig was so severely wounded that he had to retire from the 4th Dragoon service. During the battle, and the two weeks of manouvering and occasional sharp incidental skirmishing after, not even a squadron was collectively engaged.

Moylan's horse were ordered belatedly, to watch Swede's Ford and other fords upon the Schuylkill after the battle of Brandywine. Twenty of Moylan's Dragoons were sent to remove Military stores from French Creek on September 13. The next day a movement on Swede's Ford was ordered in which the 4th Dragoons took part.

Apparently, members of Moylan's 4th Dragoons were still wearing the un-dyed British red, faced with blue, uniforms and had neglected to wear the Hunting frock over them. On September 15, Lieutenant John Heard wrote Washington that he was sending in three Loyalists prisoners, who his party of Dragoons had taken because they thought ". . . we were the British Light Horse.". An event that could have been potentially dangerous for the 4th, surprisingly turned into a coup for them.

If the frustration at the lack of useful employment was galling to the 4th Dragoons, the news that soon arrived was particularly disappointing to their Colonel Moylan: On the 13, of September, Congress had commissioned Count Casimir Pulaski, Brigadier General of the Continental Light Dragoon regiments. Moylan, being the senior Dragoon Colonel, naturally resented the preference given to this foreign-voiced stranger, notwithstanding his heralded ability as a veteran cavalry leader.

The resentment grew. While Pulaski, in the three weeks before the Battle of Germantown, tried to round up the scattered detached troops of the four regiments of Continental Dragoons and form a brigade for the ensuing conflict. The various American Generals were reluctant to part with the details of Dragoons assigned to them for headquarters and orderly work. Many of the Dragoon officers, who would have preferred Moylan, a fellow American, were reluctant to take orders from Pulaski's over-bearing foreign tongued officers. Some officers actually refused to join Pulaski. Consequently, Pulaski could only muster about two hundred Dragoons from the four regiments in time for the battle.

The 4th Dragoons took part in a bit of levity between the opposing armies before the battle. When General Howe's dog wandered into the American forces while they were deploying, it was recognized as his dog by Howe's name on the collar. Washington immediately sent a trooper from the 4th Dragoons to Howe with his dog under a flag of truce, while both armies watched with many cheers from both sides.

The 4th Dragoons in Pulaski's brigade, were positioned on the extreme right of Sullivan's division. Again, the Dragoons were not effectively employed for decisive action. Unfortunately, the fog was so thick that the use of horse was not considered advisable. In the fog, quick communication on the field was impossible and the actual position of the British could not be correctly ascertained. The British were also confused in the fog, but this was unknown to the Americans, who, wary of pushing too far through a strong village, retired after a two hour battle.

Moylan and his 4th Dragoons stayed on the field with Pulaski's brigade, who were now ordered up to cover the rear-guard divisions under Greene and Stephen. Although Cornwallis relentlessly pursued them for five miles skirmishing severely with the American Light Horse. The Dragoons protective screen of the retiring American foot was so effective that Cornwallis gave up the chase.

First Lieutenant John Craig, a Pennsylvanian of the 4th Dragoons, gained recognition in the aftermath manouverings of the Germantown battle. In their first engagement with the British 16th and 17th Light Dragoons (a few horses having been found by them by this time) on a Germantown road, in a brisk melee, Craig's troop routed the British Dragoons when they came upon them in a bend of a wooded road. Several British troopers, complete with their valuable horses, arms and accoutrements, were captured. A most opportune and much needed bounty for Moylan's regiment. Lieutenant Craig succeeded to the command of his troop when his Captain, Charles Craig, was wounded, September 11, at Brandywine and left the regiment. Lieutenant John Craig led the troop until his Captaincy three months later on December 22nd.

Washington established camp on Skipback Creek for three weeks. While ther, a Court-Martial of Horse Officers, of which Colonel Moylan was President, was held at his quarters on October 16, for the trial of all prisoners of the Dragoon regiments. A week later, on the 24, the Moylan-Pulaski differences came to a head, when Moylan himself was on trial before a Court-Martial held at Upper Dublin, of which Colonel Bland of the 1st Dragoons presided. Moylan was charged with disobedience of orders of General Pulaski and of striking Pulaski's aide, Lieutenant John de Zielinski, across the face with his glove when he was disarmed and putting Zielinski under guard for delivering peremptory, and apparently conflicting, orders to Moylan from Pulaski in a most insulting manner. Moylan was also charged with ". . . giving irritating language to General Pulaski," when confronted about the affair.

Pulaski's Polish officers had little regard for American officers, who they deemed beneath them in experience. Their communication was poor, due to the language barrier. Moylan, the ranking Colonel of Horse, was not inclined to accept any un-civility from a junior officer, particularly from one of Pulaski's *Polish Usurpers.* That was not the *American way.* The Revolutionary War was being fought for freedom from this. The Continental Congress, far from the scene of war, were unaware of the difficulties involved when they dispatched their foreign proteges to the front to supercede the American officers.

The court "were of opinion that Colonel Moylan was not guilty and therefore acquited of the charge against him. On October 31, Washington approved of the verdict and ordered Moylan's "discharge from his arrest".

The affair had its epilogue though in December. Dueling was absolutely forbidden by Washington. However, Lieutenant Zielinski retaliated by "accidentally' unseating Colonel Moylan, apparently with a Polish lance, while in a drilling session. Pulaski reported the assault to Washington and sent the report by a Polish Dragoon, who had witnessed the affair and whose report favoured Zielinski. Washington was aware though, of the true circumstances. He called Zielinski before him, reprimanded him and the affair ended.

The campaign of 1777 came to a close. On the 19 of December, the 4th Dragoons moved into winter quarters at Valley Forge with Washington's army, only twenty five miles from Philadelphia.

The rigours of that hard winter added to the friction with Pulaski's Polish officers and trouble flared anew: In mid-January, of 1778, Pulaski was reporting to Washington that two of Moylan's 4th Dragoons "were wanting in respect to their officer called Tacssi, who arrested them and conducted them to his Quarters; one of them attempting to come .to me, the Officer seized the Sentry's Sword and gave the Dragoon two blows, which have maimed him. I Have arrested the Officer for his passion and particularly because he used the Sentinel's Sword, and I have imprisoned the two Dragoons.". It was apparent that the Polish-American relationship was worsening, rather than improving.

Pulaski, in spite of the arrogance of his officers, was endeavoring to effect a workable plateau with the American Dragoon Regiments. He was quick to recognize ability in the 4th Dragoon officers. When forming his troop of Lancers, he asked Washington if Captain John Craig, the hero of the Germantown Road action, might be offered the command of the new unit. Craig did not accept and the Captaincy of Lancers was given to the Lieutenant John de Zielinski of the Moylan affair.

In this first campaign of their history, the 4th Dragoons, though most effective when the opportunity was given to them, still were never allowed to employ their full potential as a complete unit. Instead, the detached troops, though in frontal service (but with numbers too meagre to be decisively effective), as was proven when the 4th Dragoons suffered the loss of three of their Captains (two of them captured, Moore Fauntleroy in the Brandywine actions and David Plunkett in the Germantown campaign. One, Charles Craig, was severely wounded at Brandywine and had to retire from Dragoon service). They were succeeded by Lieutenants George Gray, John Craig and John Heard, who were promoted to Captains.

WINTER OF 1777-1778 AND CAMPAIGN OF 1778

The harsh winter at Valley Forge saw Colonel Moylan exerting himself to re-furbish and completely equip his 4th Dragoon regiment. It was soon apparent that there would not be enough feed in the area for the horses of the Dragoon regiments and they were dispersed to be quartered in New Jersey where feed was more readily obtainable. Washington also hoped that this moving away of the American Dragoons would alleviate the Polish-American tensions, for the winter at least.

The ardous task of obtaining remounts from the wary farmers was renewed. The word soon spread that remounts were being sought and the farmers hid their best horses. Finally, horses could only be obtained by Congress calling upon each State for a quota of horses. Dragoon recruits were also in the quotas. Moylan dispatched his best officers, who were most knowledgeable in horse-flesh and horsemen, to receive them. At the appointed rendezvous, the recruits and horses met with the riding masters of each regiment and under the care of experienced officers, exercised them and prepared them to take to the field.

In March, of 1778, the Polish-American tensions eased when Brigadier General Pulaski resigned from the command of the Horse to raise his Legion Corps. Colonel Moylan, being the senior officer next in line, was appointed Brigade-Major and given the command of the 1st, the two troops of the 2nd under Tallmadge, the 3rd Light Dragoons and his own 4th Dragoons.

Moylan, though not commissioned a Brigadier General, still, had finally been given the command he sought. He quickly realized that his new status was a dubious distinction, for now he had the seemingly impossible task of outfitting and recruiting for not one, but four regiments of Light Dragoons. Moylan's Quartermaster skill came to the fore when he endeavored to establish credit with the scarce manufacturers of equipment. Not much help was obtained from Washington or Congress and it inevitably ended up with Moylan having to send his officers to the manufacturers themselves.

Much to Moylan's chagrin, as well as his hard working recruiting officers, Pulaski in recruiting for his new Legionary corps was authorized to draught from each Dragoon regiment, two troopers of his own choosing, with their horses, arms and accoutrements, as well as a sergeant from the 2nd Dragoons. Moylan must have raged inwardly at this seeming blood-letting from his command, as Pulaski only picked the very best men. The draftees as well, were not overly anxious to serve under Pulaski's foreign officers.

In the meantime, a constant patrol was maintained to watch Howe in Philadelphia. The duty fell mainly on the Pennsylvanian 4th Dragoons, they being the best acquainted with the roads into Philadelphia.

On March 20, Moylan was ordered to send a relief of his best men. The newly promoted Captain John Heard was dispatched with a detachment of the 4th Dragoons. Heard soon distinguished himself by attacking a strong foraging party from the city near Germantown. After a brisk engagement with their rear-guard, he captured several British and Loyalists, including George Spangler, a noted spy.

The 3rd of April saw a Corporal and six Dragoons of the 4th detached to escort the Commissioners arranging an exchange of prisoners.

The coming of Spring saw several Dragoon officers and troopers accused of taking furloughs without leave and galloping about the country in April, some even as far as their homes. A few of the more daring 4th Dragoons managing to slip through the British lines into occupied Philadelphia to see their families. This was necessarily accomplished while afoot, thus they were exemplifying the traditional "a-horse or a-foot" flexibility of the true Light Dragoon. However, the other more mobile self-furloughed Dragoons were reducing their horses to a worse condition than those which had been kept on duty the whole winter. Apparently, this was a result of the necessity of spreading the cavalry out so that they could obtain the necessary forage. Slackness of discipline naturally resulted in the enterprising American mind, so foreign to the strictly *levelled* British or Polish trooper. The un-authorized *movements* of the Dragoons were ended when a firm reminder was issued that any further men absent without leave would be court-martialed.

The shortage of arms for the Dragoons was as serious as the constant need for horses. When the British evacuated Philadelphia on June 18 to start their march to New York, Moylan could only arm 120 Dragoons in his brigade. Moving forward with his 120 Dragoons, Moylan harassed Clinton's marching army and watched their direction and noted their roads so that Washington could be advised and act accordingly. Lieutenant Colonel Anthony Walton White with the 4th Dragoons was sent to the rear of the army, and the remainder of the Dragoon regiments were on Clinton's front and left flanks.

Moylan posted himself on a hill with thirty of his 4th Dragoons where he had a fair view and could receive dispatches from his Dragoons of Clinton's route. He would then forward the information to Washington. The frailities of man, even an American patriot, were almost his undoing. A Trumpet-Major of the 1st Dragoons deserted to the British and notified them of Moylan's position. A large body of the now mounted 16th and 17th British Light Dragoons swept up the hill to take him, only to find that Moylan, forewarned barely in time, had moved off the hill.

Two days later, on June 28, during one of the hottest days in America, the battle of Monmouth was fought. Though actively engaged, the Continental Dragoons small dispersed numbers forebade any concentrated attack or manouvre. They did however, make it impossible for Clinton's British army to stop and pillage the country. The American Dragoons continued to harass the retreating British army all the way to Sandy Hook before they embarked for New York City. A party of Moylan's 4th Dragoons attacked part of the British rear-guard near Middletown and captured a Captain, Lieutenant, an Ensign, and two privates after a severe skirmish with them.

After British transports picked up Clinton's army at Sandy Hook and transported them safely across to New York City, Washington crossed the Hudson and ensconced his army at White Plains.

The campaign was over. The Dragoons were stationed at Middlebrook, New Jersey, to watch and impede any supplies reaching the British in New York City from the country. The milk cows of the Loyalists were rounded up by the 4th Dragoons to prevent the milk flow into New York. British foraging parties sent out to obtain hay for their cavalry were partly driven off.

The 4th Dragoons now entered upon a new and comparatively

restful and idylic existence while quartered at Middlebrook, especially their officers. They spent a great deal of their time at the manor house of Colonel Van Horne of the American Militia. Van Horne's five marriagable daughters were the focal point of the officer's new and popular campaign. The unbearable heat of the Monmouth campaign seemed far behind. The manor, set in a grove of cool trees with a green lawn running up to the house with the crickets and nightingales in chorus at night to blend a romantic mood. Here Colonel Moylan could indulge in full-dress, while he pursued the eldest of the daughters. His naturally winning affability and strikingly handsome appearance were too overwhelming for the Middlebrook beauty to withstand. The engagement which soon followed, and hastened by the excitement of the war and the romantic surroundings, led to their marriage on September 12, 1778. She was not the only victim. As a consequence of the Dragoons stationing at Middlebrook for the fall and winter, all five of the daughters of Philip Van Horne found husbands.

Van Horne radiated geniality and his house was always full, resembling very much a hotel. His fabulous dinner parties were legendary. While a loyal *Rebel,* still he did not let that stop him from entertaining officers of the enemy as well as the Americans, having two sons in the Jamaica Trade, he did not want any adverse reflections on their business. As the opposing armies moved back and forth he was visited by officers from both. In spite of all this traffic, all of his charming daughters were discerning enough to marry the American officers.

Moylan was scarcely married, when he himself was almost caught and captured. His value as a capable commander of the American horse had made him a target for a commando raid by the British partisan leader Simcoe, with a force from his Queen's Rangers (formerly led by Robert Rogers of French and Indian War fame). In October, thinking to take advantage of Moylan's romantic interlude to capture him, believing that he must be in a vulnerable position, Simcoe crossed over from Staten Island to Jersey. Arriving at the 4th Dragoons quarters at Bound Brook on a dark night, they found Moylan gone, as well as his regiment. Only two officers of the 4th, too ill to travel were found in their rooms. Wary of contagion, they were spared capture. Simcoe took their paroles instead and ordered them to mark "Sick Quarters" over the doors of their rooms. Unknown to Simcoe, Moylan and his 4th Dragoons had just been sent to Durham in Connecticut to establish their quarters for the winter.

CAMPAIGN OF 1779

July found Moylan's Dragoons ordered to the Westchester front in the neighborhood of Bedford, New York. Joining Sheldon's 2nd Dragoons and a few Light Infantry stationed there, Moylan's seniority prevailed and he commanded the whole.

The year 1779 saw the 4th Dragoons more completely uniformed and equiped in the following:

CAPS—Polished black leather with white crest and dark green turban.

HAIR—Natural color, or powdered white for dress occasions.

NECK STOCK—Black.

COAT—Dark green faced with red on the collar, lapels, cuffs, and coat tail turnbacks. Silver buttons (actually pewter). The contemporary custom would have seen the Trumpeters dressed in reverse facings, viz., a red coat with dark green collar, lapels, cuffs and coat turnbacks.

VEST—Red with small pewter buttons of silver hue.

BREECHES—Buff colored leather, or cloth.

BOOTS—Polished black with silver hued steel spurs when obtainable.

SABER AND BELT—Silver hilt with white sword knot for Troopers. Silver knot for officers. Black leather sword scabbard tipped with silver, held by a white leather belt over the right shoulder.

TROOPER'S EQUIPMENT—Black leather cartridge waist pouch. A white carbine sling over the left shoulder with silver hook to support the carbine. Carbine and pistol with reddish brown wooden parts. Metal parts and barrels of a silver hue, except the brass butt plates, trigger guard, ramrod guards and end stock cap on the pistol and carbine.

OFFICER'S EQUIPMENT—A crimson waist sash and silver epaulets. Field officer's wore epaulets on both shoulders. A Captain on the right shoulder only. Subalterns (Lieutenants and Cornets) on the left shoulder only. Field officers may also have worn the crescent shaped Gorget Officer's badge.

TRUMPETER'S EQUIPMENT—A brass trumpet with red and dark green twisted cording and tassels carried over the left shoulder. Silver epaulets on both shoulders.

HORSE EQUIPMENT—Blue-gray saddle cloth. Black leather holster with brass tips and black bear-fur covers. Saddles red-brown or black with buff hued girth. Harness, reins, headstall, breast strap, tail (crupper) strap and stirrup straps, black. Stirrups and bits, silver colour. A white picket rein was commonly used.

HORSES—Were commonly reddish-brown or darker (when obtainable). Trumpeters rode white or light-grays, or even dapple-greys.

The above complete description applied only to the 4th Dragoon troops that were completely clothed and equipped. There was a constant lack of 100% completeness of uniformity of dress and equipment in the regiment. White hunting frock shirts were still frequently worn, not to cover any un-dyed red coats, as all of the dyeing had been completed by now, but to cover the troopers unfortunate enough not to have the green coat.

While on the New England front the 4th Dragoons saw more action than they did in any other theater during the whole war. Here they encountered Tarleton, and his newly created Tarleton's Legion, Emmerich and his Loyalist Light Horse, the De Lancey Brothers and their Loyalist Horse and the veteran 17th Light Dragoons of the British line.

Almost immediately upon arriving in this new front the 4th Dragoons were engaged in action. Clinton having failed to manouver Washington into a general battle employed diverting tactics by sending marauding expeditions into New England. One of the primary raids, led by Tryon, saw the 4th Dragoons attempting to repel the British raiders. Tryon, having fired New Haven, was on his way to repeat the same havoc to Norwalk, Connecticut. From Bedford, Moylan was ordered to join General Parsons at Norwalk with his Dragoons and Infantry. Upon arrival there, Moylan found the enemy had already made good their landing and were being ineffectively repulsed by General Parson's Militia. Moylan covered the retreat of the Militia by performing as true Dragoons, in their alternate capacity as Light Infantry, by dismounting and firing from behind houses and street corners. Eventually, greatly outnumbered, Moylan was forced to order his men to retire from the town, but not before Lieutenant Erasmus Gill of the 4th Dragoons managed to take four British prisoners during the encounter.

Leaving forty Dragoons under Captain Hopkins of the 4th to harass the enemy and watch their movements, Moylan retired to Ridgefield, Connecticut. Here he rested his exhausted command from their forced march to Norwalk and prepared to join Glover's Infantry brigade on its way to assist in protecting the inhabitants of the area.

Lieutenant Colonel Anthony Walton White of the 4th Dragoons now came on stage to enhance his name as well as the regiment's fame. A diplomat as well as a successful Dragoon leader, White had been engaged in an espionage assignment for General Washington. When corresponding to him, White had presented Washington with a Bridle, Stirrups and Spurs for his horse, for which he was thanked most profusely. On August 5-6, White made a daring counter-raid within the British lines with a detachment of the 4th Dragoons and Glover's Infantry. He made a surprise attack upon the headquarters of DeLancey's Loyalist Battalions in Morrisania. He brought off thirty or more Loyalists prisoners and considerable booty before the rest escaped the main Corps. In the pursuit by the main body, White ". . . sustained a rear-guard action with spirit." DeLancey was now forced to establish his headquarters near High Bridge, closer to New York, under the guns of a British fort.

General Washington was delighted and he read White's exploit into General Orders and communicated his success to Congress.

White was rewarded on December 10, 1778. He was transferred to the Lieutenant Colonelcy of the 1st Dragoons to command them, as Colonel Bland left the service. Although a loss to the 4th Dragoons, White actively commanded the 1st Dragoons in the south.

Lieutenant Colonel Benjamin Temple of the 1st Dragoons was

transferred to the 4th on December 10, 1779, to replace White.

Besides their constant counter-harassment of the British and Loyalist to protect the inhabitants of Connecticut, Moylan employed his 4th Dragoon officers and troopers as espionage agents. They were sent into New York City and were so effective in gleaning data on Clinton's forces that they received the information only twenty four hours after Clinton himself was receiving it from his own officers. They also worked with, and in concert with Tallmadge's agent.

CAMPAIGN OF 1780

In spite of their ardous efforts to protect the inhabitants of Connecticut from marauding British and Loyalist incursions, the Governor and Assembly were opposed to the winter cantonment of Moylan's 4th Pennsylvania Dragoons at Colchester. Stating that they were a "southern regiment". A classic example of the disunity in the newly formed thirteen states. The 4th Dragoons were just as anxious to be "south" at home in Pennsylvania. They were homesick, unpaid, and their uniforms ragged and threadbare from hard campaigning. Most of the troopers' terms of enlistment were up and Moylan was hard pressed to persuade enough men to re-enlist so that he might have at least the pretence of a regiment.

Undaunted by the "foreign treatment" his 4th Dragoons were receiving from the Connecticut government, Colonel Moylan assigned Captains Pike and Craig to recruit for the regiment among the Connecticut inhabitants. They apparently were not very successful, for the strength of the regiment by April, 1780, had dwindled to eighteen, eleven of which were engaged for the war, five until April 1, one until July and one to September. Eleven were Pennsylvanians.

During the drastic reduction of the regiment, the Governor of Connecticut called on Moylan several times for Dragoons to enforce the embargo on the Loyalists on the western coast of the state to prevent them from selling supplies to the British.

June saw the departure of Moylan's 4th Dragoons from Connecticut, as well as the 2nd Dragoons. They joined Washington at

Springfield, New Jersey. At King's Ferry six troopers of the 4th with an officer were left, with orders to remain on the west side, and dispatch a Dragoon every morning with a written report of any appearance of enemy craft upon the Hudson River. The officer to come on himself with the last Dragoon.

Arriving at Washington's headquarters in Springfield, the regiment were stationed in the rear of the army with order to dispatch a patrol of fifteen men to patrol the country adjacent to the army. By July, the surprising success of Moylan's recruiting officers was apparent when the 4th Dragoons reported a strength of ninety five. The promise in March of new uniforms (caps, leather breeches, boots, swords, pistols and cartouch boxes and new saddles) finally materialized and the regiment regained a more healthy color in size and appearance.

On July 20, 1780, Moylan's 4th Dragoons of ninety five joined General Mad Anthony Wayne in the attack on the block house at Bull's Ferry near Fort Lee on the west bank of the Hudson. The objective was the *Cattle Rustling* of a large number of cattle and horses which the enemy were making ready to transport to New York. While Wayne made the diversionary feint against the block house, Moylan's Horse drove off the much needed stock, remounts for the 4th Dragoons and cattle for Washington's Army. For this coup, the British Major Andre wrote his famous *Cow Chase.*

There being no other noteworthy exploits for the year, the regiment continued in their routine patrols and orderly duties. December found them encamped in the upper part of Lancaster County still maintaining their strength of ninety five.

CAMPAIGN OF 1781

By May of 1781, the regiment were still in their Lancaster camp. At this time a number of the 4th Dragoons were involved in an attempted Gaol rescue of one of their Dragoons, who had been confined by the local militia. Assembling they marched upon the Gaol. The Militia sentry was confronted by a Dragoon with a cocked pistol, whereupon the sentry managed to fire first and killed the Dragoon. Upon falling the Dragoon's pistol went off wounding a militiaman nearby. The rescue attempt of the Gaoled 4th Dragoon came to an abrupt end, but the local litigation over the wounded militiaman was endless.

As a prelude to Washington's Yorktown campaign, a squadron of sixty officers and men of Moylan's Dragoons preceded the regiment south. They were sent to join Lafayette on the James River in Virginia to become actively engaged in the preliminary manouvering before the siege of Yorktown. Colonel Moylan and the thirty five of the balance of his 4th Dragoons remained with Washington and marched with him to Yorktown. Re-united at the Siege of Yorktown, the 4th Dragoons took the position of honour on the right of the American line.

After the capitulation of Yorktown, the 4th Dragoons, still numbering ninety four troopers and fourteen officers, were sent to reenforce General Greene arriving at his camp on January 4, 1782.

At this time the regiment lost their Colonel. Moylan had been actively campaigning for five steady years. He was forced to return to Philadelphia to recover his very poor health.

CAMPAIGN OF 1782

Five days later, on January 9, the regiment went south to Georgia with General Wayne, to establish the authority of the United States at Savannah, now that the decisive siege at Yorktown had ended the major conflict of the war.

In this last campaign, the 4th Dragoons saw some of the most gruelling service and hardest fighting of their career. They remained with "Mad Anthony Wayne" until the close of the war, repeatedly distinguishing themselves in their hard fought engagements against the British at Savannah and their Creek and Cherokee Indian allies. Two engagements were particularly noteworthy:

The British had kept fairly close within their fortifications at Savannah, not wanting to risk a confrontation with "Mad Anthony". Venturing out only once in any considerable body (approximately 440 men, including 80 Dragoons) to keep their communication (and esteem) open with a force of Creek warriors coming down to join them.

On May 20, Wayne, having been informed of General Clarke's movement, put his command in motion to intercept Clarke's force upon their return to Savannah. His vanguard consisted of Lieutenant Henry Bowyer and thirty of Moylan's 4th Dragoons and Captain Parker with sixty Light Infantry. They were ordered to force-march ahead of Wayne's army to gain possession of Baillou's Causeway. Arriving at the end of the Causeway, Bowyer and Parker, to their chagrin, discovered a patrol of cavalry before them on their side of the stream. The British Dragoon officer mistook Bowyer for an ally. He advanced in a friendly gesture, until it was too late. Bowyer and his 4th Dragoons surrounded their rear and the officer and eighteen Dragoons were taken prisoners. One Dragoon managed to break through and warn the British Colonel Brown, who was moving in column with his cavalry in front upon the causeway. Though smaller in numbers, Lieutenant Bowyer ordered a charge upon the British Dragoons who were supported by their infantry. The narrow causeway was an equalizer of numbers and Bowyer's daring charge with his 4th Dragoons threw the British Dragoons into confusion and they were thrown back upon their massed infantry on the narrow Causeway. The intensive drive of Bowyer's Dragoons forced the British back over the causeway. Five of their Dragoons were killed and some wounded, including Colonel Douglass, second in command of the British expedition. Moylan's 4th Dragoons suffered two killed and three wounded.

Although Wayne could not arrive in time to improve on the advantage Bowyer had made, still he secured all the roads to Savannah, but Brown managed to take a bye-path through a swamp and slipped back into Savannah the next morning.

The following month, in June, Chief Guristersigo set out with three hundred Creek warriors to secretly join Clarke in Savannah. En-route they learned of a small American picquet at Gibbon's Plantation which they decided to capture. Guristersigo was sadly misinformed, for the "picquet" consisted of Wayne's entire force of approximately five hundred men including Moylan's 4th Dragoons. When the Creeks attacked on the night of June 23, "Mad Anthony" personally led Moylan's 4th Dragoons upon the Creeks' left flank and after a severe conflict the Indians were routed. At the same time Wayne's infantry had charged their front at bayonet-point.

Wayne's combined attack was so effective and Guristersigo killed, his demoralized warriors returned in flight to their villages.

The Georgia campaign resolved, the 4th Dragoons returned with Wayne to Charlestown where Greene, his superior officer was-besieging Charlestown. Here they remained until December 14, when the British evacuated the city.

Besides their active campaigning, the regiment had to combat the "plague" that was prevalent during the autumnal months and which always proved disabling to un-aclamated whites on the low South Carolina coast. During the closing months of the war the regiment had shrunk to two troops, one mounted and the other dismounted, the whole commanded by Major Moore Fauntleroy and two Captains.

In July, 1783, the 4th Dragoons were furloughed and transported back to Philadelphia where they were finally mustered out, "after being received with the ringing of bells by the joyous and gratified populace."

So ended the far-flung services of "Moylan's Horse". Though stricken with the growing pains and independent individualism of the new American, *the American Patriot*. Still, many of the newly created thirteen states had benefited by their grueling campaigning. Although few in numbers, their bravery had compensated in their many unique and unequal contests in their determined efforts to share in the winning of their new country's independence.

APPENDIX I

Service Biography of all
Continental Dragoon Officers

THE FIRST CONTINENTAL LIGHT DRAGOONS:

BELFIELD, JOHN - (Va.) - Lt. of Company of Va. Light Dragoons, June 18, 1776; Captain 1st Cont. Drag., Mar. 15, 1777; Major 3rd Cont. Drag., ?, 1781; retired Nov. 10, 1782. (Name also spelled Bedfield.)

BLAND, THEODORICK - (Va.) - Captain of A Company of Va. Light Drag., June 14, 1776; Major Light Drag., Dec. 4, 1776; Colonel 1st Cont. Drag., March 31, 1777; resigned Dec. 10, 1779. (Died June 1, 1790).

BOWYER, HENRY - (Va.) - 2nd Lt., 12th Va., Nov. 15, 1777; Regimental Adjutant, Jan. 1, 1778; Regimental designated 8th Va., Sept. 14, 1778; Lieutenant 1st Cont. Drag., Feb. 18, 1781; retained in Baylor's Conso. Reg. Nov. 9, 1782, and served to close of war. (Died June 13, 1832.)

CARNE, JOHN - (S.C.) - Surgeon's Mate 1st Cont. Drag., Aug. 1777; Asst. Deputy Apothecary, Southern Dept., Sept. 20, 1781, to close of war. (Name spelled Came.)

CLEMENTS, HENRY - (Va.) - Cornet of a Co. of Va. Light Drag., June 19, 1776; Lt., 1st Cont. Drag., Feb. 20, 1777; resigned Nov. 15, 1777; Lt., 5th Maryland, Apr. 25, 1781 and served to Jan. 1, 1783.

DANDRIDGE, ALEXANDER SPOTSWOOD - (Va.) - Lt. of a Co. of Va. Light Drag., June 17, 1776; Captain 1st Cont. Drag., Mar. 15, 1777; resigned April 14, 1780.

DAVIS, THOMAS - (Va.) - Chaplain 1st Cont. Drag., Dec. 10, 1777, to ___?

DIGGES, COLE - (Va.) - Cornet 1st Cont. Drag., Mar. 31, 1777; resigned May 4, 1778.

FAUNTLEROY, GRIFFIN - (Va.) - 2nd Lt., 7th Va. Mar. 5, 1776; 1st Lt., Oct. 28, 1776; resigned Nov. 16, 1777; Cornet 1st Cont. Drag., Nov. 11, 1777, to ___? (Was in service Nov. 1778.)

GLASCOCK, THOMAS - (Ga.) - 1st Lt., Ga. Reg., July 1, 1777; Lt. 1st Cont. Drag., ___? 1779, to Nov. 10, 1782. (Died May 9, 1841.)

GRAY, WILLIAM - (Va.) - Lt., 1st Cont. Drag., ___?; was in service in 1779.

GREEN, BERRYMAN - (Va.) - Paymaster 1st Cont. Drag., with

rank of Captain Jan. 1, 1778, to ____? (Was in service Feb. 1779.)

HARRISON, CUTHBERT - (Va.) - Lt. of Va. Drag., June 15, 1776; Captain 1st Cont. Drag., Feb. 12, 1777, and served to ____?

HILL, BAYLOR - (Va.) - Cornet 1st Cont. Drag., Dec. 4, 1776; Lt., ____?, 1777 Captain, ____?, 1780; served to Jan. 1783.

HOPKINS, DAVID - (Va.) - Captain 4th Cont. Drag., Jan. 21, 1777; Major 1st Cont. Drag., ____?, 1780 and served to close of war. (Died Mar. 4, 1824.)

HUGHES, JASPER - (Va.) - Cornet 1st Cont. Drag., ____?, 1781; transferred to Baylor's Conso. Reg., and served to close of war.

HUGHTS, JOHN - (Va.) - Quartermaster-Sergt., st Cont. Drag., Feb. 1777; Regimental Qtrmstr. Dec. 27, 1777; Capt., Mar. 31, 1781; transferred to Baylor's Conso. Reg. and served to close of war.

JAMESON, JOHN - see 2nd Cont. Dragoons.

JOHNSON, WILLIAM - (Va.) - Surgeon's Mate, 1st Cont. Drag., Mar. 1778; resigned Jan. ____?, 1780.

JONES, LLEWELLYN - (Va.) - Capt. Va. Reg. of Drag., June 17, 1776; Captain 1st Cont. Drag., Mar. 31, 1777, to ____? (In service Dec. 1778.)

JONES, WILLIAM - (Va.) - Cornet of a Va. Reg. of Drag., June 15, 1776; resigned Dec. 18, 1776; 2nd Lt. of Gray's Add. Cont. Reg. Mar. 6, 1777; 1st Lt. Dec. 1, 1777; resigned Feb. 7, 1778.

LEWIS, ADDISON - (Va.) - Lt., Reg. Va. Drag., June 19, 1776; Captain 1st Cont. Drag., Mar. 15, 1777 and served to ____?

MASSEY, JOHN - (Va.) - Cornet 1st Cont. Drag., ____?, 1781; transferred to Baylor's Conso. Reg., and served to close of war.

NELSON, JOHN - (Va.) - Capt. of a Co. of Va. Drag., June 19, 1776; resigned Feb. 12, 1777.

NEVILLE, JOHN - (Va.) - Cornet 1st Cont. Drag., ____? 1780 to ____?

NIXON, HENRY - (Va.) - Private 1st Cont. Drag., Jan. 1777; Ensign, 3rd Va., Aug. 15, 1777 and served to ____?

PEMBERTON, THOMAS - (Va.) - Cornet 1st Cont. Drag., Dec. 5, 1776; Lt., ____?, 1778; Captain, ____?, 1780 and served to Jan. 1783.

PENN, WILLIAM - (Va.) - 1st Lt., Va., Drag., June 16, 1776;

Capt. 1st Cont. Drag., Nov. 25, 1776; died Mar. 15, 1777.

RICE, JOHN - (N.C.) - Adjutant 1st N, Carolina Dec. 10, 1776; Ensign, Mar. 28, 1777; 2nd Lt., Apr. 3, 1777; 1st Lt., 1st Cont. Drag., June 1, 1778 and served to ____?

ROSE, ROBERT - (Va.) - Surgeon 1st Cont. Drag., Dec. 10, 1776; retained in Baylor's Conso. Regt., and served to Nov., 1783.

SCOTT, CHARLES - (Va.) - Cornet 1st Cont. Drag., ____?, 1781; retained in Baylor's Conso. Regt., and served to close of war.

SWAN, JOHN - (Md.) - Captain 3rd Cont. Drag., Apr. 26, 1777; taken prisoner at Tappan, Sept. 28, 1778; Major 1st Cont. Drag., Oct. 21, 1780; retained in Baylor's Conso. Regt. and served to close of war.

TEMPLE, BENJAMIN - (Va.) - Capt., Va. Drag., June 15, 1776; Lt.-Col. 1st Cont. Drag., Mar. 31, 1777. Transferred to 4th Cont. Drag. Dec. 10, 1779 and served to close of war.

THROCKMORTON, ALBION - (Va.) - Cornet 1st Cont. Drag., ____?, 1781 and served to ____?

VAUGHAN, CLAIBORNE - (Va.) - Surgeon's Mate 6th Va., Nov. 1, 1776; transferred to 1st Cont. Drag., in 1779; retained in Baylor's Conso. Reg., and served to close of war.

WALTERS, JOHN - (Va.) - Cornet 1st Cont. Drag., 1781; retained in Balor's Conso. Reg. and served to close of war.

WATTS, JOHN - (Va.) - Cornet Va. Drag., June 17, 1776; Lt., 1st Cont. Drag. Dec. 18, 1776; Captain Apr. 7, 1778; wounded at Eutaw Springs, Sept. 8, 1781; retained in Baylor's Conso. Reg. and served to close of war; Lt.-Col., Light-Dragoons, U.S. Army, Jan. 8, 1799; honorably discharged, June 15, 1800. Died June 8, 1830.

WATTS, WILLIAMS - (Md.) - Cornet 1st Cont. Drag., Dec. 18, 1776; Lt., Mar. 31, 1777, and served to ____?

WHITE, ANTHONY WALTON - (N.J.) - Lt.-Colonel 3rd N.J. Regt., Jan. 18, 1776. Lt.-Colonel 4th Cont. Drag., Feb. 15, 1777; Lt.-Col. Commandant 1st Cont. Drag. Dec. 10, 1779; Colonel Feb. 16, 1780. Brigadier General U.S. Army, July 19, 1798; honorably discharged June 15, 1800. Died Feb. 10, 1803.

WHITE, GEORGE - (N.J.) - Cornet 4th Cont. Dragoons in 1778. Lt. 1st Cont. Dragoons 1780. Transferred to Baylor's Conso. Regt. and served to war's end.

WHITING, FRANCIS - (Va.) - 1st Lt. of Thruston's Additional Continental Regt., May 28, 1777; Lt., 1st Cont. Dragoons, Apr., 1779. Transferred to Baylor's Conso. Regt. and served to close of war.

WORSHAM, WILLIAM - (Va.) - Cornet 1st Cont. Drag., Feb. 4, 1778, to ____?

YANCEY, LEIGHTON - (Va.) - Lt., 1st Cont. Drag., in 1778 and served to ____?

YANCEY, ROBERT - (Va.) - Cornet 1st Cont. Drag., Mar. 31, 1777. Regimental Quartermaster, Feb. 12, 1777; Lt., ____? Captain, ____? and served to close of war. Died Nov. 17, 1824.

(Compiled from Heitman's "Historical Register of the Officers of the Continental Army", Wash., 1914; and other contemporary documentary sources.)

SECOND CONTINENTAL LIGHT DRAGOONS

BARNETT, WILLIAM - (N.J.) - Captain 2nd Cont. Drag., Jan. 15, 1777; resigned Oct. 11, 1777.

BEEKMAN, THOMAS - (N.Y.) - 2nd Lt. of Laher's Reg. New York Militia, June to Dec. 1776; Cornet 2nd Cont. Drag., Jan. 26, 1777; Lieutenant, Oct. 20, 1777; resigned in 1778.

BELDEN, EZEKIEL PORTER - (Conn.) - 2nd Lt. of Bradley's Conn. State Reg., June 20, to ____? Dec. 1776; Lieutenant 2nd Cont. Drag., Dec. 20, 1776; Captain Apr. 2, 1777; resigned June 11, 1780.

BLAGDEN, SAMUEL - (Conn.) - Major Aide-de-Camp to Gen. Wooster Sept. 17, 1775, to ____?, Dec. 1776; Major 2nd Cont. Drag., Dec. 24, 1776; Lt.-Colonel, Apr. 7, 1777; resigned Aug. 1, 1779. (Name also spelled Blackden.)

BRONSON, ISAAC - (Conn.) - Surgeon's Mate 2nd Cont. Drag., Nov. 14, 1779, and served to close of war.

BULL, AARON - (Conn.) - Fifer 2nd Conn., May 11, to Sept. 1, 1775; Sergeant 2nd Cont. Drag., Mar. 8, 1777; Lieutenant, Nov. 5, 1778; Regimental Quartermaster, Dec. 1, 1778, and served to close of war.

BULL, EPAPHRAS - (Conn.) - Was one of the party under

Arnold that captured Fort Ticonderoga, May 10, 1775; Captain Conn. Light Horse Militia, in 1776; Captain 2nd Cont. Drag., Jan. 10, 1777; Major 1st Cont. Drag., Aug. 1, 1779. Died Sept., 1781.

BURKMAN, THOMAS - (Mass.) - Cornet 2nd Cont. Drag., Jan. 26, 1777; Lieutenant, Oct. 20, 1777; resigned Aug. 20, 1779.

CRAFTS, NATHANIEL - (Mass.) - Captain 2nd Cont. Drag., Jan. 26, 1777; resigned Jan. 1, 1778.

DICKINSON, SILVANUS - (N.Y.) - Cornet 2nd Cont. Drag., Dec. 1, 1778; Lieutenant _____?, Sept., 1779; resigned Apr. 5, 1780.

DOLE, JAMES - (Conn.) - Private 2nd Cont. Drag., May 7, 1777; Sergeant, Feb. 1, 1778; Sergeant-Major, May 12, 1779; taken prisoner at Camden, Aug. 16, 1780; Cornet 2nd Cont. Drag., Jan. 14, 1781, and served to close of war.

EDGAR, DAVID - (N.J.) - 2nd Lt. of Forman's Reg., New Jersey Militia, July 1776; 1st Lt. 4th New Jersey, Nov. 28, 1776; resigned Jan. 14, 1777; Lieutenant, 2nd Cont. Drag., Jan. 25, 1777; Captain, Nov. 23, 1778, and served to close of war.

HAWLEY, GIDEON - (Conn.) - Private 2nd Cont. Drag., Apr. 16, 1777; Corporal, Sept. 16, 1777; Sergeant, Jan. 7, 1778; Quarter-Master-Sergeant, Sept. 5, 1778; Cornet, June 14, 1781, and served to close of war.

HAZZARD, SAMUEL - (N.Y.) - Lieutenant 2nd Cont. Drag., Jan. 23, 1777; resigned Dec. 25, 1777.

HOMANS, JOHN - (Mass.) - Surgeon 2nd Cont. Infantry, Jan. 1, to Dec. 31, 1776; Surgeon 2nd Cont. Drag., Dec. 18, 1776; resigned Aug. 4, 1881. (Died June 13, 1800.)

HOOGLAND, JERONIMUS - (N.Y.) - Lt. and Adjutant of Lasher's New York Militia Reg., June 1776; taken prisoner at Long Island, Aug. 27, 1776; exchanged, Jan. 1777; Lieutenant and Adjutant 2nd Continental Drag., Oct. 7, 1777; Captain, Nov. 20, 1778, and served to close of war.

HURLBUT, GEORGE - (Conn.) - Private in the Lexington Alarm, Apr. 1775; Sergeant 7th Conn., July 8, to Dec. 10, 1775; Ensign 19th Cont. Infantry, Jan. 1, to Dec. 31, 1776; Cornet 2nd Cont. Drag., Apr. 12, 1777; Lieutenant, Dec. 25, 1777; Captain, Aug. 1, 1779; wounded near Tarrytown, New York, July 15, 1781, and died of his wounds, May 8, 1783.

JACKSON, THOMAS FREDERICK - (Conn.) Cornet 2nd Cont.

Drag., Jan., 1779; Lieutenant, Nov. 15, 1779; Major and Aide-de-Camp to Gen. Alexander, July 8, 1781, to Jan. 15, 1783.

JAMESON, JOHN - (Va.) - Captain of Virginia Reg. of Drag., June 16, 1776; Major 1st Cont. Drag., Mar. 31, 1777; (transferred to 2nd Cont. Drag.?); wounded near Valley Forge, Jan. 21, 1778; Lieutenant-Colonel and transferred to 2nd D, Aug. 1, 1780, and served to close of war.

JANES, ELIHAJ - (Conn.) - Cornet 2nd Cont. Drag., Nov. 16, 1779; Lieutenant, Nov. 24, 1779; wounded and taken prisoner at Fort St. George, Nov. 23, 1780; rejoined Reg. in 1781; Regimental Paymaster, ____?, 1782, and served to close of war. (Died Feb. 22, 1823.)

JONES, JOSHUA - Cornet 2nd Cont. Drag., Nov. 16, 1779, to ____?

KING, ELIJAH - (Cornet 2nd Cont. Drag., Nov. 16, 1779, to ____?

KING, JOSHUA - (Mass.) - Cornet 2nd Cont. Drag., Nov. 16, 1779; Lieutenant, Nov. 20, 1779; wounded at Eutaw Springs, Sept. 8, 1781; served to close of war.

KINNEY, ABRAHAM - (Pa.) - Ensign 3rd Penn., May 24, 1779; Lieutenant 2nd Cont. Drag., June 14, 1781, and served to close of war.

LORING, JOSEPH - (Conn.) - Surgeon's Mate, 2nd Cont. Drag., May 1, 1777; resigned May 15, 1778.

MILLS, SAMUEL - (Conn.) - Quartermaster-Sergeant, 2nd Cont. Drag., Jan 12, 1777; taken prisoner at ____?, Dec. 14, 1777; exchanged, Aug. 8, 1780; Lieutenant 2nd Cont. Drag., to rank from June 2nd, 1778; resigned Oct. 8, 1780.

MUMFORD, DAVID - (Conn.) - Surgeon's Mate, 2nd Cont. Drag., May 16, 1778; resigned as Surgeon's Mate and appointed Lieutenant same regiment, Nov. 14, 1779; resigned June 11, 1780.

PATTON, JAMES - (Conn.) - Sergeant, 2nd Cont. Drag., Mar 22, 1777; Cornet, Oct. 11, 1777; Lieutenant, June 2, 1778; resigned May 25, 1779. (also spelled Patten and Paton.)

PIKE, WILLIAM - (Mass.) - Sergeant, 2nd Cont. Drag., Mar. 16, 1778; Cornet, June 14, 1781, and served to close of war.

POOLE, THOMAS - (Conn.) - Cornet 2nd Cont. Drag., Jan 10, 1777; Lieutenant, Apr. 7, 1777; resigned Sept. 15, 1778.

RHEA, AARON - (N.J.) - Ensign 1st N.J., Sept. 12, 1778; Lieutenant, 2nd Cont. Drag., Aug. 17, 1781, and served to close of war.

ROGERS, JEDEDIAH - (Conn.) - Cornet 2nd Cont. Drag., Feb. 15, 1778; Lieutenant, June 2, 1778, and served to close of war; Captain Light Dragoons United States Army, May 4, 1792; resigned Oct. 25, 1792.

SEYMOUR, HORACE - (Conn.) - Regimental Quartermaster, 2nd Cont. Drag., Mar. 25, 1777; Cornet, July 10, 1778; Lieutenant, June 2, 1779; and served to close of war.

SEYMOUR, THOMAS YOUNG - (Conn.) - Lieutenant, 2nd Cont. Drag., Jan. 10, 1777; Captain, Oct. 20, 1777; resigned Nov. 23, 1778.

SHELDON, ELISHA - (Conn.) - Major Commandant Battalion Conn. Light Horse, June, 1776; Colonel 2nd Cont. Drag., Dec. 12, 1776, and served to close of war.

SHETHAR, JOHN - (Conn.) - Lt., 2nd Cont. Drag., Dec. 31, 1776; Captain, Oct. 11, 1777; resigned Mar. 8, 1780.

SIMONET, JOHN - Cornet 2nd Cont. Drag., Apr. 20, 1777; Lieutenant, Jan. 1, 1778; "ran away Apr. 1, 1779."

STANTON, WILLIAM - (Conn.) - Captain of Burrall's Conn. State Reg., Jan. 1776, to Jan. 1777; Paymaster 2nd Cont. Drag., Mar. 1, 1777, to close of war; had rank of Lieutenant from Apr. 1, 1778, and Captain from Mar. 8, 1780.

STODDARD, JOSIAH - (Conn.) - Served with Ethan Allen at Ticonderoga in May, 1775; Captain 2nd Cont. Drag., Dec. 31, 1776; died Aug. 24, 1779.

TALLMADGE, BENJAMIN - (Conn.) - Adjutant of Chester's Conn. State Reg., June 20, 1776; Brigade-Major to Gen. Wadsworth, Oct. 11, 1776; Captain 2nd Cont. Drag., Dec. 14, 1776; Major, Apr. 7, 1777. By the act of Dec. 6, 1780, it was "resolved, while Congress are sensible of the patriotism, courage and perseverance of the officers and privates of their regular forces, as well as of the militia thruout these United States, and of the military conduct of the principal Commanders in both, it gives them pleasure to be so frequently called upon to confer marks of distinction and applause for enterprises which do honor to the profession of arms, and claim a high rank of military achievements; in this light they view the enterprise against Fort St. George, on Long Island, planned and conducted with wisdom and great gallantry, by Major Tallmadge, of the Light Dragoons, and executed with intrepidity and complete success by the officers and soldiers of the detachment. Ordered therefore, that Major Tallmadge's report to the Commander-in-Chief be published, with the preceding minute, as a tribute to distinguished merit, and in testimony of the sense Congress entertain of this brilliant service." Served at Gen. Washington's Headquarters, Mar., 1781, to Nov., 1783; Brevet Lt.-Colonel, Sept. 30, 1783. (Died Mar. 17, 1835.)

THOMPSON, BENJAMIN - (Conn.) - Adjutant 2nd Cont. Drag., Mar. 1, 1777; left regiment Oct. 3, 1777.

VALCOUR, JOHN SIMONET De - (France) - Cornet 2nd Cont. Drag., Apr. 20, 1777; Lieutenant, Jan. 1, 1778; brevet Captain, Dec. 1, 1778, and permitted to retire from the service.

VERNEJOUX, JEAN LOUIS De - (France) - Brevet Captain Cont. Army, Sept. 19, 1776; Captain 2nd Cont. Drag., to rank from Dec. 18, 1776; ran away Oct. 15, 1777, and was dismissed by Gen. Gates, Oct. 20, 1777.

WADSWORTH, ELIJAH - (Conn.) - Cornet 2nd Cont. Drag., Apr. 7, 1777; Lieutenant, Jan. 1, 1778; Captain, Mar. 8, 1780; retired Jan. 1, 1783.

WEBB, JOHN - (Conn.) - Lieutenant 2nd Cont. Drag., Jan. 12, 1777; Captain, Jan. 1, 1778; Aide-de-Camp to General Howe in 1781; served to close of war.

WELLS, JAMES - (Conn.) - Sergeant 2nd Cont. Drag., May 7, 1777; Cornet, Jan. 1, 1778; Lieutenant, June 2, 1779, and served to __ ?

WHETMORE, HEZEKIAH - (N.Y.) - Quartermaster 2nd Cont. Drag., Jan. 12, 1777; Adjutant of Steven's Battalion of Artillery, Feb. 1, 1777; resigned Sept. 6, 1778. (Name also spelled Wetmore.) Dep. Paymaster Gen. 1781 to close of war.

WHITING, FREDERICK J. - (Conn.) - Lt., 2nd Cont. Drag., June 14, 1781; Adjutant in 1782; retired Nov. 9, 1782.

WOODRUFF, BENJAMIN - (Conn.) - Regimental Quartermaster 2nd Cont. Drag., Apr. 5, 1777; discharged Jan. 1, 1778.

THIRD CONTINENTAL LIGHT DRAGOONS

BARNETT, CHURCHILL - Lieutenant 3rd Cont. Dragoons, Jan. 2, 1779, to ____?

BARNETT, WILLIAM - Lieutenant 3rd Cont. Drag., Apr. 10, 1778, to ____?

BARRETT, CRISWELL - (Md.) - Cornet 3rd Cont. Drag., Feb. 6, 1777; Regimental Quartermaster, Jan. 2, 1779; resigned Nov. 1, 1779 at Cowpens.

BARRETT, WILLIAM - (Va.) - 1st Lieutenant 3rd Cont. Drag., Apr. 10, 1778; Captain, ____?, May 1779; retained in Baylor's Consolidated Reg. of Drag., Nov. 9, 1782, and served to close of war.

BARRY, MICHAEL - Surgeon 3rd Cont. Drag., Nov. 1, 1779, to ____?

BAYLOR, GEORGE - (Va.) - Lt.-Colonel and Aide-de-camp to General Washington, Aug. 15, 1775, to Jan. 9, 1777. By the act of Jan. 1, 1777, it was "Resolved, that a horse properly caparisoned for service, be presented to Lt.-Colonel Baylor." Colonel 3rd Cont. Drag., Jan. 9, 1777; surprised, wounded and taken prisoner at Tappan, Sept. 28, 1778; exchanged ____? His regiment consolidated with the 1st Cont. Drag., Nov. 9, 1782; retained in command of same and served to close of war. Brevet Brig.-General Sept. 30, 1783. (Died ____? March, 1784.) After the war went to Barbadoes and died there in 1784. By act of Congress, May 25, 1832, his widow Ann Baylor, received $19,950.44 for his commertation pay as Col. of Dragoons. [Saffel's "Records of The Rev." 385.]

BAYLOLR, JOHN - (Va.) - Lt. 3rd Cont. Drag., Feb. 15, 1777; Captain, 1780, and served to close of war.

BAYLOR, WALKER - (Va.) - Lt. 3rd Cont. Drag., June 28, 1777; Captain, Feb., 1780; resigned July 10, 1780.

BELL, HENRY - (Va.) - Lt. 3rd Cont. Drag.

BELL, HENRY - (Va.) - Lt. 3rd Cont. Drag. ____? 1780, to ____? at Cowpens

BIRD, BENJAMIN - (Pa.) - 3rd Lieutenant of Thompson's Penn. Rifle Regiment, June 25, 1775; 2nd Lieutenant 1st Continental Infantry, Jan. 1, 1776; 1st Lieutenant, Sept. 25, 1776; Captain 4th

Penn., Jan. 3, 1777; Lt.-Colonel 3rd Cont. Drag., Mar. 14, 1777; resigned Nov. 20, 1778. (Name spelled Burd and Byrd.) Died Oct. 5, 1823.

CARTER, JOHN HILL - Lieutenant, 3rd Cont. Drag., Oct. 12, 1777, to ___?

CONNOR, EDWARD - (S.C.) - Cornet and riding master, 3rd Cont. Drag., July 27, 1778; Lieutenant, Dec., 1779 to ____? (Died Dec. 1836.)

DADE, BALDWIN - (Va.) - Cadet 3rd Continental Drag., May 10, 1778, to ___?

DADE, FRANCIS - (Va.) - Cornet 3rd Cont. Drag., May 1, 1778; Lieutenant, 1780, and served to ____?

EVANS, GEORGE - (Va.) - Surgeon 3rd Cont. Drag., May 20, 1777; taken prisoner at Tappan, Sept. 28, 1778; exchanged, ____?; resigned Aug. 1, 1779.

EVANS, THOMAS - (Va.) - Surgeon's Mate, 3rd Cont. Drag., June 7, 1777; resigned June 1, 1779.

FITZHUGH, _____ - Captain, killed at Old Tappan, Sept. 28, 1778.

FITZHUGH, PEREGRINE - (Va.) - Cornet, 3rd Cont. Drag., June 16, 1778; Lieutenant, ____?; appointed Lt.-Colonel and extra Aide-de-Camp to General Washington, July 2, 1781, and served as such to ___?; was also Captain 3rd Cont. Drag. ____?, and served to close of war.

FITZHUGH, WILLIAM - (Va.) - Cornet 3rd Cont. Drag., ___?, 1779; Lieutenant, ____?, 1782; transferred to Baylor's Regiment of Consolidated Dragoons, Nov. 9, 1782, and served to close of war.

GARNETT, BENJAMIN - (Md.) - Ensign 5th Maryland, Oct. 1777; Lieutenant, Oct. 13, 1778; Regimental Adjutant, Sept. 23, 1779; transferred to 3rd Cont. Drag., ____?, 1781, and served to Nov. 10, 1782.

GORDON, AMBROSE - (Va.) - Paymaster 3rd Cont. Drag., Nov. 1, 1779; wounded at Eutaw Springs, Sept. 8, 1781; retained in Baylor's Consolidated Reg. Nov. 9, 1782, and served to close of war.

HARRIS, JOHN - (Va.) - Ensign 1st Va., Feb. 11, 1781; 2nd Lieutenant, Sept., 1781; transferred to Baylor's Consolidated Regiment, Nov. 9, 1782, and served to close of war.

HART, BENJAMIN - Cornet and Regimental Quartermaster 3rd Cont. Drag., July 26, 1778 to ____?

HITE, GEORGE - (Va.) - Ensign 8th Va., Sept. 10, 1780; transferred to 3rd Cont. Drag., Aug., 1782; Lieutenant, Oct. 1782, and served to close of war.

JONES, CADWALLADER - (Va.) - Captain 3rd Cont. Drag., Feb. 6, 1777 to ____?

JONES, CHURCHILL - (Va.) - Captain 3rd Cont. Drag., June 1, 1777; transferred to Baylor's Consolidated Reg., Nov. 9, 1782, and served to close of war.

LEWIS, FIELDING - (Va.) - Captain in 1777?

LEWIS, GEORGE - (Va.) - Lt. Commander in Chief's Guard and aide to Washington in 1776; Captain 3rd Cont. Drag., Jan 1, 1777, and served to close of war.

MERIWETHER, JAMES - (Va.) - Adjutant 1st Va. State Reg., Feb. 1778, to Oct. 1779; Cornet 3rd Cont. Drag., ____? 1780; Lieutenant, ____?, 1781; retained in Baylor's Consolidated Reg., Nov. 9, 1782, and served to close of war.

MORROW, _____, - Lieutenant, wounded at Tappan, Sept. 28, 1778.

NELSON, ROGER - (Md.) - 2nd Lieutenant 5th Maryland, ___?, 1779; 1st Lieutenant, July 15, 1780; wounded and taken prisoner at Camden, Aug., 1780; exchanged Dec., 1780; transferred to Baylor's Reg. Cont. Drag., Nov. 9, 1782, and served to close of war. (Died June 7, 1815.)

PAGE, CARTER - (Va.) - 1st Lieutenant 3rd Cont. Drag., Jan. 8, 1777; Captain, Apr. 10, 1778; Aide-de-Camp to General Lafayette, June to Nov., 1781; served to close of war. (Died Apr., 1825.)

PARSONS, WILLIAM - (Va.) - Cornet 3rd Cont. Drag., Feb. 6, 1777; Lieutenant, Jan. 1, 1779; Captain, Nov., 1779; retained in Baylor's Cons. Reg., Nov. 9, 1782, and served to close of war.

PERRY, JOHN - Cornet 3rd Cont. Drag., ____?, 1781; retained in Baylor's Conso. Reg., Nov. 9, 1782; served to close of war.

RANDOLPH, CHARLES - (Va.) - Cornet 3rd Cont. Drag., Feb., 1777; Lieutenant, June 14, 1777, and served to ____? (In service, Jan., 1780.)

RANDOLPH, ROBERT - (Va.) - Cornet 3rd Cont. Drag., Feb.,

1777; Lieutenant, June 14, 1777; wounded and taken prisoner at Tappan, Sept. 28, 1778.

SIMMONS, _____ - Cornet (at Cowpens - Eutaw).

SIMONS, _____ - Lt. (Eutaw) from S.C. Dragoons.

SMITH, ROBERT - Captain 3rd Cont. Drag., Jan. 9, 1777, to ___? (Was in Service Jan., 1780.)

STEWART, PHILIP - (N.J.) - Lieutenant 3rd Cont. Drag., ___?, 1780; wounded at Eutaw Springs, Sept. 8, 1781; transferred to Baylor's Conso. Reg., and served to close of war; Lieutenant 2nd Artillerists and Engineers, June 5, 1798; resigned Nov. 15, 1800. (Died Aug. 14, 1830.)

SWAN, JOHN - (Md.) - Captain 3rd Cont. Drag., Apr. 26, 1777; taken prisoner at Tappan Sept. 28, 1778; Major 1st Cont. Drag., Oct. 21, 1780; retained in Baylor's Conso. Reg., and served to close of war.

TEAS, WILLIAM - (Md.) - Cornet 3rd Cont. Drag., 1779 to 1781. (Died 1824.)

THORTON, PRESLEY PETER - (Va.) - Cornet 3rd Cont. Drag., Feb. 21, 1777; Lieutenant ____?; Lt.-Colonel Aide-de-Camp to General Washington, Sept. 6, 1777, to ____?; Captain, ____?, and served to June, 1783; Captain 8th United States Infantry, Jan. 10, 1799; honorably discharged, June 15, 1800.

WALLACE, JAMES - Lieutenant 3rd Cont. Drag., in 1780.

WALLACE, JAMES - (Va.) - Surgeon 2nd Va., June, 1777; Surgeon 3rd Cont. Drag., 1778; retained in Baylor's Conso. Reg., and served to close of war.

WASHINGTON, WILLIAM AUGUSTINE - (Va.) - Captain 3rd Virginia, Feb. 25, 1776; wounded at Trenton, Dec. 26, 1776; Major 4th Cont. Drag., Jan. 27, 1777; Lt.-Colonel 3rd Dragoons, Nov. 20, 1778; wounded at Cowpens, Jan. 17, 1781. By the act of Mar. 9, 1781, it was "Resolved, that a medal of silver be presented to Lt.-Colonel Washington of the Cavalry, with emblems and mottoes descriptive of his conduct at the battle of Cowpens, Jan. 17, 1781." Wounded and taken prisoner at Eutaw Springs, Sept. 8, 1781, and was a prisoner on parole to close of war; Brig.-General United States Army, July 19, 1798; honorably discharged, June 15, 1800. (Died Mar. 6, 1810.)

WATTS, JOHN - (Va.) - Cornet Va. Drag., June 17, 1776; Lt.,

1st Cont. Drag., Dec. 18, 1776; Captain Apr. 7, 1778; wounded at Eutaw Springs, Sept. 8, 1781; retained in Baylor's Conso. Reg., and served to close of war; Lt.-Colonel, Light-Dragoons, U.S. Army, Jan. 8, 1799; honorably discharged, June 15, 1800. Died June 8, 1830.

WOOLFOLK, WILLIAM - Lieutenant and Regimental Quartermaster 3rd Cont. Drag., 1779, to ____?

CLOUGH, ALEXANDER - (N.J.) - Adjutant 1st New Jersey, Nov. 20, 1775; Major 3rd Cont. Drag., Jan. 8, 1777; killed at Tappan, Sept. 28, 1778.

FOURTH CONTINENTAL LIGHT DRAGOONS

BIRD, WILLIAM - (Pa.) - 1st Lt., 2nd Penn. Battalion, Jan. 5, 1776; taken prisoner at Three Rivers, June 8, 1776; exchanged ____?; Captain 4th Cont. Drag., Jan. 10, 1777; resigned July 8, 1778.

BOWEN, JOHN - Cornet 4th Cont. Drag., Oct. 12, 1778, to ____?

CATHCART, WILLIAM - Surgeon 4th Cont. Drag., Apr. 1, 1777; resigned May 1, 1778.

COBURN, JOHN - Cornet 4th Cont. Drag., Jan. 10, 1777, to ____?

CRAIG, CHARLES - (Pa.) - 1st Lt., of Thompson's Penn. Rifle Reg., June 25, 1775; Captain, Nov. 9, 1775; Captain 1st Cont. Inf. Jan. 1, to Dec. 31, 1776; Captain 4th Cont. Drag., Jan. 10, 1777; wounded at Brandywine, Sept. 11, 1777, and did not rejoin army.

CRAIG, JOHN - (Pa.) - 2nd Lt., 2nd Penn. Battalion, Jan. 5, 1776; 1st Lt., 3rd Penn. Nov. 11, 1776; 1st Lt., 4th Continental Drag., Mar. 22, 1777; Captain, Dec. 22, 1778 (or 1777?), and served to close of war. (Died Nov. 29, 1829.)

CROSS, WILLIAM - (Pa.) - 3rd Lt., of Thompson's Penn. Rifle Reg., June 25, 1775; 2nd Lt., 1st Cont. Inf., Jan. 1, to Dec. 31, 1776; 1st Lt., 4th Cont. Drag., Jan. 1, 1777; Captain 4th Penn. June 3, 1777; resigned May 14, 1778.

DORSEY, LARKIN - (Md.) - 2nd Lt. Baltimore Artillery Co., Nov. 5, 1776; Cornet 4th Cont. Drag., Jan. 25, 1777; resigned Sept.

4, 1778.

DORSEY, RICHARD - (Md.) - 3rd Lt., of Richardson's Maryland Battalion of the Flying Camp, Sept. 17, to Dec. 1, 1776; Lt., 4th Cont. Drag., Jan. 24, 1777; Resigned Apr. 15, 1778; Captain Independent Co., Maryland Artillery, May 4, 1777; company attached to and formed part of the 1st Cont. Artil. May 30, 1778; wounded and taken prisoner at Camden, Aug. 16, 1780; prisoner on parole to close of war.

DORSEY, THOMAS - (Pa.) - Capt. 1st Penn. Battalion Oct. 27, 1775; 2nd Penn. Oct. 25, 1776; resigned Jan. 1, 1777; Captain 4th Cont. Drag., Jan. 10, 1777; omitted Aug. 1777.

FAUNTLEROY, MOORE - (Pa.) - Captain 4th Cont. Drag., Jan. 21, 1777; taken prisoner, Sept. 25, 1777; Major, Aug. 1, 1779, and served to ____? (Was in service Jan. 1780.)

FELL, WILLIAM E. - Cornet 4th Cont. Drag., Feb. 10, 1777; omitted Mar. 1778.

FRANK, LAWRENCE - (Pa.) - 1st Lt., 4th Cont. Drag., Oct. 1, 1779; Captain, ____?, 1782, and served to ____?

FUNK, JACOB - (Pa.) - Ensign 4th Penn. Battalion, Jan. 8, 1776; Cornet 4th Cont. Drag., Jan. 10, 1777, and served to ____?

GILL, ERASMUS - (Va.) - Sergt. 2nd Va., Aug. 28, 1776; Ensign, Nov. 28, 1776; 2nd Lt., June 15, 1777; 1st Lt., 4th Cont. Drag., Feb. 1779, to rank from Dec. 25, 1778; taken prisoner at the Siege of Savannah, Oct. 3, 1779; exchanged Oct. 22, 1780; Captain, ____?, 1781, and served to close of war.

GRAY, GEORGE - (Va.) - Ensign 3rd Va., May 8, 1776; Lt., 4th Cont. Drag., Jan. 10, 1777; Captain, Dec. 7, 1777; resigned May 1, 1779.

GUTHRIE, GEORGE - (Va.) - Cornet 2nd Cavalry Pulaski Legion, July, 1779; Lieutenant 4th Continental Dragoons ____? and served to close of war.

HALLETT, JONAH - (N.Y.) - Ensign N.Y. Militia Reg., June 18, 1776; 2nd Lt., of Malcolm's Add. Cont. Reg., July 26, 1777; resigned Apr. 23, 1779; Lt., 4th Cont. Drag., Oct. 2, 1779, and served to Nov. 1782.

HEARD, JOHN - (N.J.) - Lt., 4th Cont. Drag., Jan. 20, 1777; Captain Feb. 8, 1778, and served to close of war.

HENDERSON, JOHN - (Pa.) - Cornet, 4th Cont. Drag., Jan. 20,

1777; Regimental Quartermaster, July 1778; omitted Sept. 1778.

HENDERSON, WILLIAM - (Pa.) - Lt., and Regimental Paymaster 4th Cont. Drag., Feb. 22, 1777; resigned May 31, 1780.

HOPKINS, DAVID - Captain, 4th Cont. Dragoons.

HORD, JOHN - (Va.) - Lt., 4th Cont. Drag., Jan. 20, 1777, to ___?

HOWARD, VASHEL D. - (Va.) - Captain 4th Cont. Drag., Jan. 24, 1777; died Mar. 15, 1788.

McCALLA, THOMAS H. - (Pa.) - Surgeon's Mate, 4th Cont. Drag., May 1, 1778; Surgeon, June 1, 1780, and served to Nov. 1782.

McCAWLEY, THOMAS H. - Surgeon's-Mate 4th Cont. Drag., May 1, 1778; Surgeon June 1, 1780, to ____?

MANIFOLD, PETER - (Pa.) - Cornet 4th Cont. Drag., Apr. 14, 1778;; Lt., May 1, 1778; Captain, Aug. 1, 1779; resigned Oct. 30, 1780.

MOORE, NICHOLAS RUXTON - (Md.) - 2nd Lt., of Fulford's Co., Maryland Cannoneers, Mar. 1776; Lt., 4th Cont. Drag., Feb. 2, 1777; Captain, Mar. 15, 1778; resigned Dec. 31, 1778. (Died Mar. 9, 1816.)

MOYLAN, STEPHEN - (Pa.) - Muster-Master-Gen. Cont. Army, Aug. 11, 1775; Aide-de-Camp to Gen. Washington, Mar. 6, 1776; Colonel Quartermaster Gen., June 5, 1776; resigned as Quartermaster-Gen., Sept. 28, 1776, but remained on staff of Gen. Washington until appointed Colonel 4th Cont. Drag., Jan. 5, 1777, and served to Nov. 3, 1783; brevet Brig.-Gen., Nov. 3, 1783. (Died Apr. 11, 1811.)

OVERTON, THOMAS - (Va.) - 2nd Lt. 9th Va., Aug. 14, 1776; 1st Lt. Mar. 9, 1778; transferred to 1st Va., Sept. 14, 1778; Lt., and Adjutant 4th Cont. Drag., July 1, 1779; Captain, Apr. 24, 1781, and served to close of war.

PEYTON, DADE - (Va.) - Cornet 4th Cont. Drag., Mar. 2, 1779; Lt., June 2, 1779, and served to ____?

pike, zebulon - (N.J.) - Cornet 4th Cont. Drag., Mar. 1, 1777; Regimental Adjutant, Nov. 20, 1777; Lieutenant, Mar. 15, 1778; Captain, Dec. 25, 1778; Regimental Paymaster, June 1, 1780, and served to close of the war; Captain in the Levies in 1791; Captain U.S. Infantry, Mar. 5, 1792; assigned to 3rd Sub Legion, Sept. 4,

1792; assigned to 3rd Infantry, Nov. 1, 1796; Major, Mar. 21, 1800; transferred to 1st Infantry, Apr. 1, 1802; brevet Lt.-Colonel, July 10, 1812, honorably discharged June 15, 1815. (Died July 27, 1834.)

PLUNKETT, DAVID - (Md.) - 2nd Lt., of Smallwood's Maryland Reg., Jan. 14, to Dec., 1776; Captain 4th Cont. Drag., Jan. 10, 1777; taken prisoner, Oct. 20, 1777, at ____?; resigned Mar. 1, 1779.

SULLIVAN, JOHN - (Pa.) - Cornet 4th Cont. Drag., ____?; Lt., Oct. 1, 1779; "left the service without leave before the conclusion of the war;" see Jrn. Cont. Cong., June 27, 1786.

THOMPSON, JOSEPH - (Pa.) - Surgeon's Mate, 4th Cont. Drag., June 1780, and served to close of the war.

TRENT, LAWRENCE - (Va.) - Cornet 4th Cont. Drag., ____?, 1778; Lt., and Regimental Quartermaster, Oct. 1, 1779; Captain, ____?; served to close of war.

WILLIAMSON, SAMUEL - Chaplain, 4th Cont. Drag., May 1, 1778; omitted May, 1779.

WILLIS, HENRY - (Pa.) - Cornet 4th Cont. Drag., June 1777; Lt., Dec. 22, 1778; Captain, Dec. 22, 1780; resigned Apr. 24, 1781.

ROBBINS, JOHN - (Va.) - Lt., 4th Cont. Drag., Oct. 1, 1781, and served to close of war.

TEMPLE, BENJAMIN - (Va.) - Captain, Va. Drag., June 15, 1776; Lt.-Colonel 1st Cont. Drag., Mar. 31, 1777; transferred to 4th Cont. Drag., Dec. 10, 1779, and served to close of war.

WHITE, ANTHONY WALTON - (N.J.) - (See 1st Cont. Dragoons.)

WHITE, GEORGE? - (Cornet, 4th Cont. Dragoons.

(The above biographical service sketches of all of the officers of the four regiments of the American Continental Light Dragoons for the American Revolutionary War are a most valuable compilation for the Geneologist as well as Historian.

The sketches were compiled from Heitman's "Historical Register of the Officers of the Continental Army" and other contemporary documentary sources.)

The First and Third
Continental Light Dragoons Consolidated:

November 9, 1781.

Sir: -

Pursuant to the orders of Major-General Greene, of the 2nd and 3rd days of November, 1782, we have formed the 1st and 3rd Regiments of Dragoons, now serving in the State of South Carolina, into five Troops, agreeably to an order of the Secretary of War, to be commanded by the following officers:

George Baylor, Colonel, commissioned January 8, 1777.
William Washington, Lieutenant-Colonel. (On Parole, to end of war.)
John Swan, Major, commissioned October 21, 1780.
Churchill Jones, Captain, commissioned June 1, 1777.
John Watts, Captain, commissioned April 7, 1778.
William Barrett, Captain, commissioned May, 1779.
William Parsons, Captain, commissioned Nov., 1779.
John Hughes, Captain, commissioned March 31, 1781.
Ambrose Gordon, 1st Lieut., commissioned Dec., 1779.
John Linton, 1st Lieut., commissioned May, 1780.
Henry Bower, 1st Lieut.
Francis Whiting, 1st Lieut.
Chas. Yarborough, 1st Lieut.
James Merriweather, 2nd Lieut.
John Harris, 2nd Lieut.
Goerge White, 2nd Lieut.
Philip Stewart, 2nd Lieut.
William Fitzhugh, 2nd Lieut.

_____Nelson, Paymaster.
Charles Scott, Cornet.
Hasper Hughes, Cornet.
John Massey, Cornet.
John Perry, Cornet.
John Walters, Cornet.
Robert Rose, Surgeon.
John Wallace, Surgeon.
_____Vaughn, Surgeon's Mate.

Doctor Rose being sick at present, and unable to do immediate duty, Doctor Wallace is arranged to do the duty of Surgeon to the regiment until the recovery of Dr. Rose.

It is the opinion of the Board that a Court of Inquiry be, as soon as possible, ordered to determine the rank of the officers, to the end that the dates of their commissions may be inserted in the arrangement. We have arranged the officers of the 1st and 3rd regiments to a command in the five troops, in proportion to the number of troops in each corps, from the principle of their being entitled to promotion regimentally.

Your obedient servants,
Anthony Wayne, B.G.
John Swan, Major L.D.
Churchill Jones, Captain L.D.

APPENDIX III

Tables of Battles & Actions of Continental Light Dragoons

The First Continental Light Dragoons: (See text for losses)

Battle or Action (American victories have asterisks*	Date	American Commander	First Dragoons Commander	British or Loyalist Commander
1-Woodbridge (NJ)	6/24/77		Bland	
2-Short Hills (NJ)	6/28/77	Stirling	Bland	Cornwallis
*3-Lee's 1st Action (Pa)	9/77	Lee	Lee	
4-BRANDYWINE (Pa)	9/11/77	Washington	Bland	Howe
*5-Lee-Hamilton Exploit (Pa)	9/77	Lee	Lee	
6-GERMANTOWN (Pa)	10/4/77	Washington	Bland	Howe
*7-Whitemarsh (Pa)	12/7-8/77	Washington	Bland	Howe
*8-Scott's Farm (Pa)	1/20/78	Lee	Lee	Simcoe
9-Haddonfield (NJ)	3/78	Wayne	Pulaski	
*10-MONMOUTH (NJ)	6/27/78	Washington	Bland	Clinton
11-Savannah (Ga)	10/9/79	Lincoln	Pulaski Temple	
12-Monk's Corner (SC)	4/14/80	Huger	Jameson	Tarleton
*13-White's Santee Foray (SC)	5/6/80	White	White	
*14-Lenud's Ferry (SC)	5/6/80	White	White	Tarleton
GREENE'S SOUTHERN CAMPAIGN:				
*15-Cowpens (SC)	1/17/81	Morgan	Capt. Watts	Tarleton
16-Wetzell's Mill (NC)	3/6/81	Greene	Watts	Cornwallis
17-Guilford (SC)	3/15/81	Greene	Watts	Cornwallis
18-Hobkirk's Hill (SC)	4/25/81	Greene	Watts	Rawdon

*19-Santee Raids (SC)	7-8/81	W. Washington	Watts	
*20-Eutaw Springs (SC)	9/8/81	Greene	Watts	Stewart
*21-Siege of Charleston (SC)	81-82	Greene		Stewart
LAFAYETTE'S VIRGINIA CAMPAIGN:				
*22-Spencer's Ordinary (Va)	7/26/81	Butler	McPherson	Simcoe
23-Green Springs (Va)	7/6/81	Wayne	McPherson	Cornwallis
*24-YORKTOWN (Va)	9/28-10/19/81	Washington	White	Cornwallis
*25-White's Chattahoochee Raid (Ga)	9/24/82	White	White	

The Second Continental Light Dragoons: (See text for losses)

Battle or Action (American victories in *Asteriks)	Date	American Commander	Second Dragoons Commander	British or Loyalist Commander
*1-TRENTON (NJ)	12/26/76	Washington	Bull & Seymour	Rall
*2-PRINCETON (NJ)	1/3/77	Washington	Bull & Seymour	Cornwallis
3-Woodbridge (NJ)	6/24/77	Moylan	Tallmadge	
4-Short Hills (NJ)	6/28/77	Stirling	Tallmadge	Cornwallis
5-BRANDYWINE (Pa)	9/11/77	Washington	Tallmadge	Howe
6-GERMANTOWN (Pa)	10/4/77	Washington	Tallmadge	Howe
*7-SARATOGA (NY)	9/19, 10/7, 10/17/77	Gates	Seymour	Burgoyne
*8-Whitemarsh (Pa)	12/7-8/77	Washington	Tallmadge	Howe
9-Rawdon's Action (Pa)	12/77	Tallmadge	Tallmadge	Rawdon
*11-Jameson-DeLancey Action (NY)	2/2/78	Jameson	Jameson	DeLancey
*10-The Rising Sun Caper (Pa)	12/77	Tallmadge	Tallmadge	17th L.D.
12-Clap Tavern Road (NY)	10/7/78			
*13-Poundridge (NY)	7/2/79	Sheldon	Sheldon	Tarleton
14-Tryon's Norwalk Raid (Conn)	7/79	Moylan	Sheldon	Tryon
*15-Morrisania (NY)	8/5/79	White		DeLancey
*16-Lloyd's Neck (NY)	9/5/79	Tallmadge	Tallmadge	
*17-Ft. St. George (NY)	11/23/80	Tallmadge	Tallmadge	
*18-Corum (L.I., NY)	11/23/80	Tallmadge	Tallmadge	

*19-Ft. Knyphausen (NY)	7/2/81	Lauzun	Sheldon	DeLancey
*20-Tarrytown (NY)	7/15/81	Sheldon	Sheldon	British Navy
*21-Ft. Slongo (L.I., NY)	10/3/81	Trescott	Hulbert	
*22-Norwalk Is. (NY)	12/7/82	Brewster	Sergt. Churchill	
*23-Capture of the "Shuldham"	1/83	Tallmadge	Tallmadge	
*24-Stratford Pt. Naval Coup	2/20/83	Brewster	Rhea-Stanley	Capt. Hoyt

The Third Continental Light Dragoons: (See text for losses)

Battle or Action (American victories *Asteriked)	Date	American Commander	Third Dragoons Commander	British or Loyalist Commander
1-GERMANTOWN (Pa)	10/4/77	Washington	Baylor	Howe
*2-Cooper's Ferry (NJ)	5/4/78	Maj. Clough	Clough	17th L.D.
3-Barren Hill Church (Pa)	1778	Lt. Carter	Carter	
*4-MONMOUTH (NJ)	6/28/78	Washington	Bird	Clinton
5-Old Tappan (NJ)	9/27/78	Baylor	Baylor	Grey
*6-Rutledge's Plantation (SC)	3/26/80	W. Washington	W. Washington	Tarleton
*7-23rd Mile House (SC)	4/5/80	W. Washington	W. Washington	Brit. Leg.
8-Monck's Corner (SC)	4/14/80	W. Washington	W. Washington	Tarleton
*9-Wambaw Plantation (SC)	5/6/80	White	W. Washington	Brit. Leg.
10-Lenud's Ferry (SC)	5/6/80	White	W. Washington	Tarleton
11-Waxhaws (SC)	5/29/80			Tarleton
*12-Rugeley's Farm (SC)	12/4/80	W. Washington	W. Washington	Rugeley
*13-Hammond's Store (SC)	12/29/80	W. Washington	W. Washington	Waters
*14-Ft. Williams (SC)	12/29/80	Simmons	Simmons	Cunningham
*15-COWPENS (SC)	1/17/81	Morgan	W. Washington	Tarleton
16-Wetzell's Mill (NC)	3/6/81	Greene	W. Washington	Cornwallis
17-GUILFORD (SC)	3/15/81	Greene	W. Washington	Cornwallis
18-HOBKIRK'S HILL (SC)	4/25/81	Greene	W. Washington	Rawdon
*19-Santee Raids (SC)	7-8/81	W. Washington	W. Washington	
*20-EUTAW SPRINGS (SC)	9/8/81	Greene	W. Washington	Stewart
*21-SIEGE OF CHARLESTON (SC)	81/82	Greene	Capt. Parsons	Stewart

The Fourth Continental Light Dragoons (See text for losses)

Battle or Action (American victories *Asteriked)	Date	American Commander	Fourth Dragoons Commander	British or Loyalist Commander
1-Woodbridge (NJ)	6/24/77	Moylan	Moylan	
2-Short Hills (NJ)	6/28/77	Stirling	Moylan	Cornwallis
3-Cornwallis' Probe (Pa)	9/8/77	Moylan	Moylan	Cornwallis
4-BRANDYWINE (Pa)	9/11/77	Washington	Moylan	Howe
*5-Heard's Deception Coup (Pa)	9/15/77	Lt. Heard	Heard	Loyalists
6-GERMANTOWN (Pa)	10/4/77	Washington	Moylan	Howe
*7-Germantown Road (Pa)	10/77	Lt. Craig	Craig	16/17th L.D.
*8-Capture of Spangler (Pa)	3/78	Lt. Heard	Heard	
*9-MONMOUTH (NJ)	6/28/78	Washington	Moylan	Clinton
*10-Middletown (NJ)	6/29/78	Moylan	Moylan	
11-Tyron's Norwalk Raid (Conn)	7/11/79	Moylan	Moylan	Tryon
*12-Morrisania (Mass)	7/5-6/79	White	White	DeLancey
*13-Bull's Ferry (NJ)	7/20/80	Wayne	Moylan	
*14-YORKTOWN (Va)	9/28-10/19/81	Washington	Moylan	Cornwallis
*15-Baillou's Causeway (Ga)	5/20/82	Wayne	Lt. Bowyer	Brown
*16-GURISTERSIGO'S DEFEAT (Ga)	6/23/82	Wayne	Lt. Bowyer	Guristersigo

APPENDIX IV

The Establishment of the Continental Dragoons;

As passed by Congress May 27, 1778.

RESOLVED, that a battalion (regiment) of Cavalry shall consist of —

Pay per month.	Pay per month.
1 Colonel .... Dollars 93 3/4	6 Trumpeters .... each 10
1 Lieutenant Colonel . Dollars 75	12 Sergeants .... each 15
1 Major .... Dollars 60	30 Corporals .... each 10
6 Captains .... each 50	374 Dragoons .... each 8 1/3
12 Lieutenants .... each 33 1/3	1 Paymaster from the line., and
6 Cornets .... each 26 2/3	to receive in addition to his
1 Surgeon 60	pay in the line, per month . 25
1 Surgeon's Mate 40	1 Adjutant from the line, addi-
1 Saddler 11	tional pay per month 15
1 Trumpet-major 11	1 Quartermaster from the line,
6 Farriers .... each 10	add pay per month 15*
6 Quartermaster's Sgt. . each 15	

There were to be six troops to a regiment with 62 dragoons to a Troop, 1 Trumpeter, 2 Sergeants, 5 Corporals, 1 Quartermaster Sergt., 1 Farrier, 1 Cornet, 2 Lieutenants, 1 Captain per Troop. A total of 76.

A field officer was to command two troops, which was to be a squadron. Three squadrons to a regiment. A squadron to be 152 Rank and file.

The total establishment of a Dragoon Regiment was to be 468, Rank and file. But the Regiments of Dragoons never equaled more than half their authorized strength and it was more like one third or even one fifth, the strength of the famous 3rd Continental Light Dragoons in the Southern Campaigns with Greene, never exceeded 80 or 90 men.

The officers and men of a Dragoon Regiment received about 25 percent more in salary than those of a infantry Regiment. That is when they did get paid. Which, as is commonly known, was not very often.

Other Cavalry officers were to receive the following pay:

Brigadier-General of Cavalry . . . 156 1/4 per month. (There was only one Brigadier-General of Cavalry and that was Count Casimer Pulaski who resigned on March 28, 1778, after being seven months Chief of the Dragoons. Upon resigning he raised his "Pulaski Legion" and still held his rank and pay of Brigadier-General.)

A Riding-master of Cavalry was to receive 33 1/3 Dollars per month.

*Rec. of Rev. War, Saffell, W. T. R. Pages 375-76.

Sources and Textual Notes

PART ONE   THE FIRST CONTINENTAL LIGHT DRAGOONS

Principal Sources were:

ANBUREY, Lieutenant Thomas: Travels, Volume II.
BLAND, Colonel Theodorick: The Bland Papers, ed. by C. Campbell, Petersburg, Va., 1840.
BOYD, Thomas: Light Horse Harry Lee, N.Y., 1931.
DOUWES, William F.: Logistical Support of The Continental Light Dragoons, *in* Military Collector & Historian Jrn, Winter, 1972, pages 101-106.
GERSON, Noel B.: Light Horse Harry . . , Doubleday, N.Y., 1966.
GRIFFIN, I. J.: Stephen Moylan, Philadelphia, 1909.
HEITMAN, F. B.: Historical Register of the Officers of the Continental Army, Washington, 1914.
JOHNSTON, H. P.: Lafayette's Southern campaign.
JRNS (Va.): Journals of The Council of the State of Virginia, Richmond, 1931-1932, Volumes I and II.
JRNS of CC: Journals of the Continental Congress, Ford, ed., Wash., 1904-34.
KAPP: Life of Steuben.
LEE, Harry: Memoirs, Philadelphia, 1812.
LEFFERTS, Charles: Uniforms of American, British, French & German Armies in War of the American Revolution, A. J. Wall, ed., N.Y., 1926.
LOESCHER, Burt Garfield: Bland's Virginia Horse, The Story of the First Continental Light Dragoons, *in* Mil. Coll. & Hist. Jrn., VI, nl, pp. 1-6.

LONG, Sergt. John: Orderly Book, Virginia State Library, Archives Division.

McCRADY, Edward: History of South Carolina in the Revolution 1775-83.

MARSHALL: Life of Washington, Volume IV.

RISLEY, Clyde A. & William Imrie: Series 71-74, Plate 25, U.S.A. (Colonial) 1st Continental Dragoons (Bland's) ca. 1778-80.

SIMCOE, John G.: Military Journal, N.Y., 1844.

SPARKS, J.: Writings to George Washington, Volume V.

TARLETON, Banastre: History of the Campaign of 1780-81, Dublin, 1787.

TUCKER, Glenn: Mad Anthony Wayne and the New Nation, Stackpole, Pa., 1973.

LAFAYETTE: Unpublished Letters of Lafayette.

WHITE, Anthony Walton: Memoir, by A. M. Woodhull.

WISTER, Sally: Journal of Miss Sally Wister, Pa. Mag. of Hist. & Biog., 1885, page 321.

WRITINGS WASHINGTON: Writings of Geoge Washington, Vol. 10-25, J. C. Fitzpatrick, ed., Washington, 1931.

WRITINGS G. W. CALENDAR: Calendar of the Correspondence of George Washington with the officers, 4 vols., J. C. Fitzpatrick, ed., Washington, 1915.

ZLATICH, Malko: Uniforming the 1st Regiment of Continental Light Dragoons, 1776-79, *in* Military Col.. & Historians Jrn., Summer 1968, pages 35-39.

Bland's six troops of Virginia Dragoons, although not fully equipped at the outset, still were uniformed. Evidence shows that Bland's first squadron of three troops were clothed in blue coats faced with red. Lee's troops of the first (Bland's) squadron were noted by a Quaker girl as being in ". . blue and red . ." in 1777.

Captain (later Lieutenant Colonel) Benjamin Temple's second squadron of three troops wore brown coats faced with green. Evidence shows the squadron still in that color in June, 1778, for Sally Wister notes that a troop Captain, Alexander Spotswood Dandridge, wore his hair ". . . powder'd very white, a (pretty colored) brown coat, lapell'd with green and white waistcoat."

All troops of both squadrons preferred and wore brown (buff) leather breeches and high top boots (Prussian Dragoon type) when obtainable. Their Dragoon caps were of brown jacked-leather with flowing white horsehair crest surmounting the top. However, Colonel Bland reported a dearth of these on December 11, 1776, as well as boots, spurs, cartridge boxes and holsters. As late as April, 1777, Bland was berating his officers for their neglect of the appearance of their troopers, who were in sharp contrast to the officers who were always turned out well. Captain Light Horse Harry Lee, for example, wore a high frilled stock, tight lambskin breeches. In camp he was attended by a body servant and in the field he drank from silver cups. Finally, Bland's marked esprit de corps surfaced when he compiled the following incredibly detailed description of his regiment's uniform which was to be the model for the regiment's procuring officers:

"Regimental Order, April 13th 1777
Uniform of 1st Regt of Light horse Commanded by Colonel Bland
Coats Brown faced with green interrupted lapell to have a gold Vellum button Hole and yellow Buttons with the figur of a Horse and No. 1 Cast in the Button. Green Collar and Hanglar Turnup at the Bottom with a Button Hole on Each side Turnup with Vurlum Button Holes on Each Pocket. Coats Short, wests coats green with Flaps with waist Beltt plain leathor Buff Breeches. Field Officers Gold Epquletts Strop and rose without Fringe on Each Shoulder. Capt. one Gold Epaulette on the right Shoulder and plain gold Strop on the Reight. Staff Officers, Surgion, Adjutant, Paymaster, Regt. Quartermaster, a plain gold strap on Each Shoulder. Quartermaster Sargant a strop and Rose. The Colour of the facing On the right and Strop of the same Colour on the left Edged with yallow Binding. Sargants, a Strap and rose of the same Colour of the facing on the right Shouldr and a strap on the left the rose fringed with yallow worsted fringe. Corporals, a rose and Strop and fringe the Colour of the facing on the left Shoulder and plain Green Strap on the right. Rank and File, green strap on Each Shoulder. All Non-Commissioned Officers, Except Trumpet Major, Trumpetters Farrier and Sadlars and rank file, brown faced with green, interrupted lapells yallow Bind-

ing. Buttons, with the figure of a Horse No. 1 on the Buttons. Trumpet Major, green faced with Brown, two brown straps and Rose with Yellow Edging yellow bound Button Holes. Trumpetters, green faced with Brown [lined out in original] fringe Hanging from the Shoulders. Farrier and Sadler, plain Brown with green lapellets interrupts.

All Non Commissioned Officers and Rank and file whose coats are brown are to have green Hearts on the Elbow and those whose Cotes are green are to have Brown Hearts plain green westcoats and leather Breeches for all non Commissioned Officers and rank and Turnup Tops the Boots, Swoards, Belts and sling; white Caps with purpendicular fronts green lashes and yallow Fassels Holster Caps plain leather and No. 1 Marked on them. Trumpet flags the Colour of the Ridgmantal Facings.

THEODORICK BLAND''

(Note: A minimum of punctuation - commas and periods, has been done in editing to render the above a less confused series of clauses.)

Colonel Bland's priceless Uniform Orders, the only such document of any of the four Continental Light Dragoon Regiments, is preserved in First Dragoon Sergeant John Long's (of Captain John Belfield's troop) Orderly Book of 1777.

Though Bland's orders could never be completely implemented, still, they were the guide for the First Dragoon officers in their constant, if not frustrating, attempts to uniform the Regiment.

As to arms: the Regiment had joined Washington in December 1776 with insufficient quantities of carbines and "pairs of pistols", but most Troopers were armed with "spears" and tomahawks. After 1777, the Regiment received some more carbines in May 1778 and new recruits received "swords from Hunter's Manufactory in Virginia". When more carbines were not forthcoming, the balance of the Regiment were equipped with short muskets with a sling which General Know had procured from the "Eastward".

The complete his "Uniform Order" plan, Colonel Bland dispatched Lieutenant Colonel Benjamin Temple to the Regiment's allocated procurement zone in February 1778 to seek clothing from the Continental stores in Williamsburg. Temple made a successful procurement with Colonel William Finnie, the Virginia department Quartermaster General. Arrangements were consumated for sufficient cloth for Brown coats faced with Green (to comply with Bland's Uniform Orders). However, it was over six months before any finished uniforms were seen. In the interim, many of the First Dragoons were literally in rags. Major John Jameson in July 1778, after the battle of Monmouth, was pleading with Colonel Bland: ". . Our men are so naked that it is a shame to bring them into the field; pray send some officer with clothes for the poor fellows . .".

Colonel Bland was in utter frustration when he realized that his dream of completing his "Uniform Orders" were disapating into thin air. In June, 1778, he learned that Quartermaster Finnie had disposed of ". . a considerable part of the Cloathing . ." to others that he had agreed to supply Temple with. However, Bland's hopes received a reprieve. By August, Lieutenant Colonel Temple was stating that sufficient quantities of clothing was on its way of every article (but no color stated but apparently brown faced with green with red.) ". . to completely cloath every man in the Regiment, except Boots, they may want a few pair . . . and I doubt not but they will be as well equipt as Col. Moylands or Col. Sheldons Regts, . . .".

However, all of the troops of Bland's First Dragoons, were not "as well equipt" by January 1779, for *Amburey,* in his "Travels", portrays a graphic, though somewhat satirical, description of the two troops of the First Dragoons with Bland that escorted the Saratoga Convention prisoners to Virginia in 1779. *Anburey* states that Bland was proud of his Dragoons. He reviewed and manouvered them every morning: ". . it is really laughable to see him thus attended with his ragged regiment, which looks to borrow Shakespear's idea, as if the gibbets had been robbed to make it up, then the Colonel himself, notwithstanding his martial spirit, has all the grave deportment, as if he was going to a consultation.", with two troopers before and two behind him, bearing drawn swords. "as to those troops of Colonel Bland's Virginia regiment with Washington's army, I cannot say anything, but the two that the Colonel has with him here, for the purposes of expresses and attendance, are the most curious figures you ever saw; some, like Prince Prettyman, with one boot, some hoseless, with their feet peeping out of their shoes; others with breeches that put decency to the blush; some in short jackets, some in long coats, but all have fine dragoon caps, and long swords slung round them, some with holsters, some without, but gadamercy pistols, for they have not a brace and a half among the, but they are tolerably well mounted." (Anburey's letter from Jones Plantation, near Charlottesville, Virginia, 20 January 1779.)

Colonel Bland retired the same year on 10 December without realizing the fullfillment of his admirably conceived plan of uniforming his Regiment. It took a successor, Lieutenant Colonel Anthony White, to complete his dream. In a different color, not brown faced with green, but blue faced with red, but actually, the original color of Bland's own squadron. By 1781, White's squadron of the First Dragoons in Virginia, received the new uniforms from France, as well as steel or brass helmets, turned up at the base with black bearskin and long flowing horsehair crests of white (admirably portrayed by Frederick P. Todd's plate, see *Loescher,* page 3).

The fighting dress of Captain Watss' company of the First Dragoons with William Washington in Green's southern army had deteriorated to coarse white linen slip-on rifleman's jackets, somewhat shorter than the longer infantry hunting type fringed jacket, as they would be inconvenient in the saddle. Watts' company had originally obtained the "rifleman's jackets" enroute to South Carolina in 1780 with Lieutenant Colonel Temple, from secret stores that First Dragoon procurement officers had cached away in Winchester, to avoid a repeat performance of a Quartermaster Finnie "displacement".

(The principal sources for the above analytical uniform disertation to supplement the text descriptions were: *Anburey, Bland, Boyd, Douwes, Griffin, JRNS (Va.), JRNS of CC, Lefferts,* p. 64 shows a plate of Bland's own troop, *Loescher,* for a shorter history of the Regiment, page 3 is F. P. Todd's excellent plate depicting both the 1781 French type helmet as well as an American manufactured leather cap with iron bands criss-crossing the crown occasionally worn by the Regiment. The crossed iron bands offering protection to the head, particularly from sabre cuts.; *Long, Risley,* for his spirited detailed action plate; *Lafayette, White, Wister, Writings Washington, Zlatich,* for a fine study of 1780.

155

See Bibliography of First Dragoons for full titles of key words cited above: *Loescher,* etc.) ******

Captain "Light Horse Harry" Lee's troop of Bland's Virginia Horse were the "eyes" of General Washington as well as the provider of sustaining food for the dwindling American army during the winter of "76-77". Lee and his troop (with the second and third troops) preceded Colonel Bland to the Jersey front by three months. From his arrival in Washington's camp in October 1776 to the end of the year Lee and his troop executed fifteen recorded raids on the convoys of British supply wagons with the total loss of only two troopers wounded and one horse shot. Lee had honed his raids to a pre-determined science that was almost phenomenal, so successful was he. His troop for the most part comprised young dare devils even younger than Lee's twenty years. Lee had no formal military training but he was a natural military cavalry leader, which his son, Robert E. Lee later inherited. "Light Horse Harry's" early, as well as later successes were all based on his thorough reconnaissance work. His troop of young able men were capable of moving quickly. Successive strikes instilled confidence in this, the elite troop of Bland's regiment. Lee's troopers had unquestioned faith in his uncanny ability. They knew that his homework was thorough, that his knowledge of the enemy's strength and deployment was complete. Even his superiors were aware of his keen ascertainment: General Greene remarked —

"Captain Lee and I spent an evening discussing the waging of the war, and I envy his sure grasp of the essentials. I must study plans of campaigns and of battles before I know how to act, but he needs only to glance at a map of the situation to be guided, surely and accurately, by a marvelous instinct, . . ".

Lee's troop were the best equipped and uniformed unit of Bland's Virginia Horse. Funds from the Lee family fortune were the principal source for the blue coats faced with red as well as other essentials. An auxiliary weapon tucked into their cavalry boots was the long-handled hunting knife used by the frontiersmen from the Virginia-Kentucky frontier. Captain Lee and his officers were particularly eye-catching in short blue capes lined in buff colored silk. By the time that Bland's regiment of horse had gained Continental Line status on March 31, 1777, the troop's blue coats were quite threadbare from continually active service. When the troop managed to capture forty British carts laden with bolts of scarlet cloth intended for enemy uniforms attempts were made by Lee's officers to dye the wool blue but to no avail, so a quantity of much needed blankets were made from the wool cloth.

There was a strong camraderie in the troop. The closeness of age and vigour of youth was the common meld. Captain Lee and his Lieutenant were the same age of twenty, the two Cornets were eighteen and seventeen. Several troopers were in their late teens, the youngest were sixteen year old twins. The *senior* member was the twenty-four year old sergeant-major. They all owned their own splendid mounts and were excellent horsemen. Lee had trained them well, particularly in the use of the sabre. He had them practice charging at full gallop to cut down targets tied to oak tree branches.

Though of a common eager spirit to do battle or thwart the enemy, the men still did not resent their Captain's infrequent discipline. When fist fights broke out on two occasions between Lee's troopers and some Militia in Washington's camp, Lee mustered his troop and passed out his unique discipline. Not mentioning the fights, Lee ordered his Sergeant-Major to distribute thistles to every trooper who was not in the fights. As the guilty members saw the troopers proudly wearing the thistles in their Dragoon caps, they were chastised enough to thereafter keep the peace.

Although they were young and eager, Lee and his troop were not foolhardy. Lee concedes in his *Memoirs* that he learned his cavalry techniques from the British officers he fought against, namely Tarleton and the troop commanders of the 16th and 17th Light Dragoons. When possible he avoided the total impact of a frontal charge. He learned and improved on the cavalry charge. He would, before closing within the enemy's pistol range, divert to a flanking movement, thus confusing his enemy long enough to equalize the usual disparity of numbers. The British invariably outnumbering Lee's troop.

Lee and his troop were actually a principal food provider for Washington's starving army for more than two years (October 1776 through 1778). He invariably would strike a British food convoy at dusk and "cut and run" before the enemy cavalry rear-guard could come up. His first *holdup* netted twenty-one wagonloads of flour and sacks of jerked beef, a most welcome sight to Washington's hungry army.

Less than three days later he again returned, this time with seventeen wagons loaded with dried beef. The American army were quick to adopt Lee and his troop as their champions, who were able to do what they were unable to, to sting the enemy and provide them with sustaining food as well.

The very sight of the handsome, successful Lee inspired them: Washington's aide, Alexander Hamilton expressed it well -

"Captain Lee warms the blood of the footsore more than would casks of brandywine or rum . . ".

Lee and fifteen of his troop made the pre-attack reconnaisance of Trenton for Washington and recrossed the Delaware after eying the situation. However, much to Lee's chagrin, his troop was not re-ferried across to take part in the attack.

Lee and his troop continued their "requisitioning" of British food supplies for Washington's 76'-77' hungry winter army. He became most adept at striking the small outposts that were the provisioning life-line to Howe's forces in New York City. In February they managed to *relieve* the enemy of supplies from three different posts in three successive days: Newark, N.J., Perty Amboy, and Highlands on the beach.

Lee's first action of consequence since the new status of Bland's Virginia Horse as The First Continental Light Dragoons on March 31, 1777, occurred in June when Howe was manouvering before his movement to Philadelphia. He sent Cornwallis on a raid across the Raritan near the village of Millstone Creek. Lee's troop was assigned to Lincoln's corps and they managed to disperse a whole battalion of British in the action at Short Hills.

On August 28, when Howe finally landed in Maryland, Lee had his first decisive action against British cavalry, as related in our text. All the American generals and officers were cognizant of his uncanny prowess. Even Knox, the Artillerist commented:

"I have had several discussions of our campaign with Capt. H. Lee, of Virginia, a learned fellow who displays much knowledge of the maneuvers . . . of Cornwallis' cavalry screen.

I . . . believe that unless our tribulations sap his buoyancy, he will become a valued colleague.".

Lee's engagement on August 28, with the battalion of 16th and 17th Light Dragoons was particularly noteworthy. The full three troops of British outnumbered Lee's troop by almost five to one. Posting his troop behind trees, Lee awaited until one half of the British cavalry had passed by then ordered his men to fire. Thirty British Light Dragoons fell, all but three being killed. Lee then charged the cut off troop in the rear and captured the Captain and 23 men before the eyes of the other half of the British cavalry who had passed by and were afraid to fire for hitting the captured troop. When they did recover from their surprise and charge, Lee and his troop had disappeared into the woods with their prisoners, to arrive back to the American army with only one First Dragoon slightly wounded.

As the campaign of 1777 closed and Washington went into winter quarters at Valley Forge Lee and his troop resumed their depredations on British supply trains to feed the starving Americans. He accompanied General Greene on a foraging expedition into New Jersey and evoked the following discernment from the admiring Greene:

"The captain's instinct is as sure and swift as that of the eagle that drops out of the skies to snatch its prey. No convoy within range of his horses is safe from his depredations . .".

Lee not only conducted his own successful raids, he also was instrumental in preventing British foraging parties from pillaging the American farmers, much to Howe's dismay who commented in tone:

"An American named Lee, is a damned nuisance! I except the rebels to nip at our heels, but this fellow always draws blood.".

From their headquarters at Scott's Farm, six miles from Valley Forge, Lee's troop made daily forays for food for Washington's army. As a result of their enterprising efforts the Americans managed to survive the winter to be able to confront the British the following spring at Monmouth and drive them back to New York. In February 1778, Lee's troop even managed to "rustle" several hundred head of cattle to feed Washington's hungry army at Valley Forge.

Lee and his troop could be defined as a model and an example of the best of the troop units from the Continental Light Dragoon Regiments. Not that the other three Regiments did not have their own "Lees", still, their troop officers did not equal the reknown of "Light Horse Harry". *******

The charge of the First Continental Light Dragoons at Savannah in Pulaski's "Light Brigade" of 200 cavalry was comparable in a minor way to the charge of the British Light Brigade at Balaklava many decades later, with similar disastrous results. There was a conflict of plans between the American and French commands. D'Estaing insisted on a frontal attack later after he had refused Lincoln an earlier attempt, when the British were less prepared to resist an assault. The plan of assault was accordingly arranged. It was to be made on the redoubts at the north part of the British lines.

Pulaski's "Light Brigade" of his Legion Lancers and Dragoons and the First Continental Light Dragoon Regiment, in all, 200 cavalrymen, were given their orders for the assault:

"The cavalry under the command of Count Pulaski will parade at the same time with the infantry, and follow the left column of the French troops, and precede the column of the American light troops; they will endeavor to penetrate the enemy's lines between the battery on the left of the Spring Hill redoubt and the next towards the river."

They were then to pass to the left, and secure such parties of the enemy as might be lodged in that quarter.

The charge of Pulaski's Light Brigade was doomed before they started. A sergeant deserted from the American army on the evening after the order for the attack was given out and the British General Prevost had time to make the best deployment of his defenses. All attacking columns met a murderous fire. Pulaski at the head of his "Light Brigade" encountered a withering cross fire as they charged between the redoubts in their attempt to get into

160

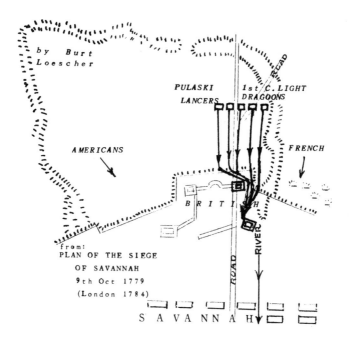

by Burt
Loescher

PULASKI
LANCERS

1st C. LIGHT
DRAGOONS

AMERICANS

FRENCH

BRITISH

from:
PLAN OF THE SIEGE
OF SAVANNAH
9th Oct 1779
(London 1784)

ROAD

RIVER

S A VA NN A H

the rear of the enemy. Pulaski himself was mortally wounded while charging at full gallop and died two days later. Repulsed on all sides in every point of attack after they had stood the British fire for fifty-five minutes, the American and French troops were ordered to withdraw.

The Light Brigade of cavalry suffered heavily and were mere remnants after Pulaski's brave, but foolhardy frontal charge. His Lancers, in the front line with Pulaski, suffered terrible losses.

This was the most noteworthy cavalry charge of the complete regiment of the First Continental Light Dragoons.

Our overlay from the official map of the attack depicts the point of attack, the surrounding hills in their 'valley of death', and the point of deadly cross fire as the cavalry attempted to 'flank through' between the redoubts.

Unfortunately, the First Dragoons did not have a contemporary poet laureate to herald the bravery of their charge in Pulaski's "Light Brigade" at Savannah. Alfred Tennyson existed in the wrong era to bestow the same fame that he gave the 17th Light Dragoons (then Lancers) for their incredible charge in the Crimea.
****

PART TWO
THE SECOND CONTINENTAL LIGHT DRAGOONS

Principal Sources were:

BOLTON, Rev. Robert: History of Westchester, Vol. II, p. 118 for the Poundridge Raid.

BRONSON, Deacon Isaac: Of Southington, Conn., Diary, *in* History of Wolcott, page 289, Orcutt, 1874.

COLLINS, J.F.: Whaleboat Warfare in Long Island Sound, *in* N.Y. History, Vol. 25, April 1944, pp. 195-200.

CONN MEN REV: Connecticut Men in the Revolution, p. 271 for Sheldon's Connecticut Horse in Saratoga campaign.

DOUWES, William F.: Logistical Support of The Continental Light Dragoons, *in* M. C. & Hist. Jrn., Winter 1972, pp. 101-106.

EPPERSON, Glen I., & Simpson, James P.: The American Revolutionary War, Battle order of cavalry, Part I, *in* Daughters of the American Revolution Mag., Nov. 1968, pp. 823-824.

FITZPATRICK, John C.: The Spirit of the Revolution, pp. 190-204, The Story of the Purple Heart, Sergeant Elijah Churchill of the 2nd Dragoons, was the first of the only three Revolutionary war soldiers to receive the Purple Heart.

FITZPATRICK, John D.: editor. The Writings of George Washington, Bicentennial Commission Edition, 26 Vols., Wash., 1931.

GRAYDON, Alexander: Memoirs of His Own Time, Philadelphia, 1846.

HAYES, John T.: The Connecticut Light Horse, *in* Mil. Coll. & Hist. Jrn., Winter, 1970, pp. 109-112.

HEATH, Major General William: Memoirs of the American War, N.Y., 1904.

HEITMAN, Francis B.: Historical Register of the Officers of the Continental Army, Washington, 1914.

JRNS CC: Journals of the Continental Congress, Ford, ed., 31 vols., 1904.

KILBOURNE, P. K.: Sketches and Chronicles of the town of Litchfield, Connecticut, 1859.

LANCASTER, Bruce: The Secret Road, Atlantic, Little, Brown. A fascinating historical novel of Tallmadge and his Secret Service.

LEFFERTS, Charles M.: Uniforms . . . . Amer. Rev. . . , N.Y., 1926.

LOSSING, B. J.: Pictorial Field Book of the Revolution, 2 Vols., 1860.

LYMAN, Daniel: Diary (unpublished), January 1-July 20, 1780.

MATHER: The Refugees of 1776 from Long Island to Connecticut.

MILLS, B. H.: Troop Units at the battle of Saratoga, in N.Y. State Historical Assoc. Qrt., Jrn., Vol. 9, Apr, 1828, pp. 136-158.

MOORE, Frank: Diary of the American Revolution, 2 Vols., N.Y., 1860.

PENNYPACKER, Morton: General Washington's Spies, L. I. Hist. Soc., 1939.

RISLEY, Clyde A. and Wm. Imrie: Series 71-74, Plate 26, 2nd Continental Dragoons (Sheldon's), 1779-81.

SEC. SERV. REV.: Secret Service of the Revolution, in Mag. Amer. Hist., Feb., 1882.

SCHERMERHORN, F. E.: American & French Flags . . Rev . . , pp. 75-9, Philadelphia, 1948.

STRYKER, W. S.: The Battles of Trenton and Princeton, Bost.-N.Y., 1898.

TALLMADGE, Colonel Benjamin: Memoirs of Colonel Benjamin Tallmadge Prepared by himself at the Request of his Children, N.Y., 1858, and 1904, The Gilliss Press. A prime source for 2nd Dragoons.

WALDO, _____: Diary, in Historical Mag., June, 1861, p. 169: ". . the confusion arising from similarity of the cloaks of the Connecticut Light Horse to that of the enemy.".

WARE, Thomas A.: The Revolution in The Hudson Highlands, Hope Farm Press, 1974.

Now that our Bi-Centennial celebration of the American Revolution is upon us, there is a striking similarity in the instability of "the American dollar" two hundred years ago and now. Which reflected most detrimentally to the raising and maintenance of Washington's four regiments of Continental Light Dragoons. The parallel is quite apparent: Basically stated, Congress having resolved to raise an army to break free from the mother country, found it was necessary to take care of the army's needs; and since the country was poorly supplied with hard cash, an effort was made to replace real cash by a fictitious money. Consequently paper money was introduced, better known as the "Continental Dollar". This was the only alternative that the Continental Congress had as it would have been extremely unwise to pay the expenses of the war by means of duties and taxes, as these had been the straws that broke the camel's back, with the mother country. The first two years of the war twenty million dollars circulated for a long time without undue depreciation and kept the American army going for the campaigns of 1776 and 1777. The dove of peace still not in sight Congress floated a new issue of bills. They still did not dare to tax the people to raise money. From then on, the "Continental Dollar" began to hastily depreciate. The following is a scale of depreciation:

Towards the middle of 1777: 2 to 3 percent loss.

The end of 1777: 2 or 3 dollars for one.

In 1778: 5 or 6 for one.

In 1779: 27 or 28 for one.

The first 4 or 5 months of 1780: 50 to 60 for one.

Soon after in 1780: 150 for one dollar.

Then in 1781: The bills were generally refused everywhere.

From 1779 on, the Continental Light Dragoon Regiments (as well as the rest of the American Continental Army) started to find that it was necessary to impress everything that was necessary to keep them in the field, clothing, food, weapons, gunpowder, horses, etc. The pressure was somewhat relieved when it was finally agreed that the States would take care of the men from their State. Connecticut, in the case of Sheldon's Second Dragoons. But, as noted in the text, this was frustratingly time consuming and if the particular Regiment had men from other states in their ranks, there was continual dissension over payment. *******

It is interesting to note that the Dragoon officers from the two Virginia Regiments (1st and 3rd) refer to Sheldon's (2nd) and Moylan's (4th) as being the best uniformed prior to 1781. The fact that Boston (the free city), in the procurement zone for the 2nd and 4th, was available, made it less harrowing for Sheldon's procurement officers. *******

164

Graydon, in his "Memoirs" gives a first hand description of the nucleous of Sheldon's Horse who gave Washington his needed reconnaisance in his dangerous 1776 retreat from New York: "Men, beyond the meridian of life, without uniformity of clothing and discipline, and armed mostly with fowling pieces . .". The handful that remained (after the enlistments were up) to serve with Washington at Trenton and Princeton were the younger hard core members who formed the nucleous of Sheldon's newly raised Second Continental Light Dragoons. *******

Major Benjamin Tallmadge was an incredible figure and ranks with any of the American heroic leaders. He was born on Long Island, New York, in 1754. As a boy he became acquainted with all of the small ports, coves and inlets, which stood him in such good stead for his many Long Island raids wit his Second Dragoons. A Yale graduate in 1773, he then became superintendent of a Connecticut school. He joined the Connecticut Militia regiment of Colonel Chester in 1775 as Adjutant and was at the battle of Brooklyn. Before his regiment was disbanded, he had the offer of the first troop in Sheldon's newly formed Second Continental Light Dragoons. Promoted to Major on April 7, 1777. Although his background had fitted him as Washington's chief spy under the code name of "John Bolton", still, it did not hamper his vigorous activities and exploits as an active Dragoon officer.

Tallmadge married immediately after the war in 1784. He served in Congress from Connecticut from 1800 to 1816, and died at the age of 81 in 1835. *******

In 1778, the 2nd Dragoons received a foreign infusion of "Horse Furniture" as a result of the old Rogers Rangers, John Stark's victory and capture of the Brunswick Dragoons at Bennington. These German heavy Dragoon type saddles were a most welcome relief to Colonel Sheldon who was striving to adequately "seat his Dragoons".-*Fitzpatrick,* Washington Writings, X, 246, Jan. 21, 1778 to commanding officer at Albany, N.Y.

PART THREE
THE THIRD CONTINENTAL LIGHT DRAGOONS

Principal Sources were:

ALLAIRE, Lieutenant Anthony: Diary.

BASS, Robert D: The Green Dragoon - The Life of Banastre Tarleton . . . , Henry Holt, N.Y., 1957. This admirable work was a prime source for the Third Dragoons in the south offering much new light on the diasters at Monck's Corner, Lenud's Ferry and American victory at Cowpens, much of it based on the unpublished Cornwallis-Tarleton Correspondence.

BAUER, Frederic Gilbert: Notes on the Use of Cavalry in the American Revolution, *in* Cavalry Journal, XLVII, 1938, pp. 136-143.

BAYLOR, O. Walker: Baylor's History of the Baylor's, LeRoy, Illinois, LeRoy Journal Printing Company, 1914.

BOATNER, III, M. M.: Landmarks of the American Revolution, pp. 185-187, Stackpole Books, Harrisburg, Pa., 1973.

CARRINGTON, H. B.: Battles of The American Revolution, N.Y., 1888.

COWPENS: The Battle of King's Mountain . . . and of the Cowpens, Wash., 1828.

DAVIS, Burke: The Cowpens-Guilford . . Campaign, Lippincott, Philadelphia, 1962.

DAWSON, H. B.: Battles of the American Revolution, 'The Massacre at Old Tappan', pp. 450-452, N.Y., 1858.

FITZPATRICK, John C., ed.: The Writings of George Washington, 39 Vols. Wash., 1931-1944. Prime Source of Dragoon officer Corr.

FITZPATRICK, John C., ed.: Calendar of the Correspondence of George Washington . . . with the officers. A prime source.

GRAHAM, James: The Life of General Daniel Morgan, 1856.

GODFREY, C.E.: The Commander in Chief's Guard. (Capt. George Lewis' Troop. Other Dragoon Regiment units also served at various times.) Washington, D.C., 1904.

GREENE, Francis Vinton: The Revolutionary War . . . , N.Y., 1911. An excellent battle source. The fine battle maps show the geodetic elevations.

JOHNSON, William: Sketches of the Life and Correspondence of Nathaniel Greene, Major General of the Armies of the U.S. in the War of the Revolution, 2 Vols., DaCapo Press, 1974, NYC. A prime source for the southern campaigns.

LEE, Henry: Memoirs of The War in The Southern Department of the United States, N.Y., 1869, Chapter XXIII for Cowpens.

LEFFERTS, Charles M.: 'Cowpens, January 17, 1781' painting, in possession of Rodman Wanamaker family.

LIEBY, A.: The Revolutionary War in the Hackensack Valley, in M.C. & Historian Jrn., Volume VI, No. 1.

LOESCHER, Burt G.: Bland's Virginia Horse . . . , in M.C. & Hist. Jrn., VI, n. 1, p. 1-6.

LOSSING, B.J.: Field Book of The Revolution, 2 vols., 1860.

MARSHALL, John: The Life of George Washington, 1804. One source for the Colonel Washington-Tarleton Cowpens duel.

MILES, W. P.: Washington Light Infantry, Proceedings at the inauguration of the monument erected at the memory of Colonel Washington at Magnolia Cemetery, May 5, 1858, Charleston, S.C., Steam Power Press of Walker Evans & Co., 1858, 42 pages.

NEWSOME, A. R., ed.: A British Orderly Book, Aug. 1780-Mar. 20, 1781, in N.C. Hist. Rev., IX, 57-58; 163-186; 273-98; 366-92 South campaign.

N.Y. GAZETTE & WEEKLY MERCURY: No. 1407, Oct. 5, 1778; No. 1409, Oct. 19, 1778.

PETERSON, H. L.: The Book of The Continental Soldier, Stack-pole, Pa., 1968.

RISLEY, Clyde A. and William Imrie: Series 71-74, Plate 27, U.S.A. (Colonial): 3rd Continental Dragoons (Baylor's), 1777-79.

ROBERTS, K.: Battle of Cowpens: The Great Morale Builder, Doubleday, 1958.

ROBERTS, Kenneth: '900 Men Who Shook An Empire' (Battle of Cowpens), in Colliers Magazine, 1956.

SCHERMERHORN, Frank E.: American . . . Flags of The Revolution, Phil., 1948.

SELLERS, Charles Coleman: Portraits and Miniatures by Charles Willson Peale, Trans. the Amer. Philosophical Soc., New Series XLII, 1952.

SEYMOUR, William: Sergeant-Major, Del. Regt. 'A Journal of Southern Expedition, 1780-83', *in* Pa. Mag. Hist. & Biography, 1883.

STRYKER, W. S.: The Massacre near Old Tappan, Read before the N.J. Historical Soc., Jan. 23, 1879, 12 pp., Trenton, 1882.

TARLETON, Banastree: History of the Campaigns of 1780-81 in the Southern Provinces of N. America, Dublin, 1787. A prime source.

WARD, Christopher: The Delaware Continentals, 1776-1783, Historical Society Delaware, 1941, Chapter 42, 'The Battle of Cowpens'.

Lieutenant Colonel William Washington, cousin to George Washington, was born in 1752, a Virginian, son of Baily Washington, of Stafford County, and was educated for the ministry. However, the start of the Revolution saw him entering the Third Virginia Infantry of General Mercer's brigade as a captain. He was wounded in the battle of Brooklyn, but distinguished himself at Trenton, where he and his Lieutenant, James Monroe (later president), were both injured in the capture of a Hessian battery on King Street.

As Lieutenant Colonel commanding the Third Dragoons in the south, he met, and became engaged to Jane Elliott, daughter of Colonel Charles Elliott, owner of 'Sandy Hill' plantation near Charleston, S.C. On one of his visits he expressed his need for a flag, or Regimental standard for his Regiment. Miss Elliott cut a square of crimson silk from the end of a rich damask curtain and fashioned it into a flag, which, being mounted on a hickory pole, became famous at Cowpens, and Hobkirk's Hill and Eutaw Springs where it derived its name, 'Eutaw Flag' in honor of the Third Dragoons gallant but futile charges and the capture of their Colonel, William Washington.

Washington married Miss Elliott in 1782 and settled in Charleston. He was later elected and served in the South Carolina legislature and was urged to run for Governor, but declined, insisting that 'he could not make a speech'. In the quasi-war with France in 1798, he served on his cousin George's (Washington) staff as a brigadier-general. William Washington died in 1810. (*Lossing,*

Miles, Schermerhorn.)

Many stories derived from Washington's duel with Tarleton at the battle of Cowpens. In the presence of the daughters of Colonel Montfort in North Carolina, Tarleton made disparaging remarks about Colonel Washington as an illiterate fellow, hardly able to write his name. "Ah, colonel," said one of the sisters, "you ought to know better, for you bear on your person proof that he knows very well *how to make his mark.*" (referring to Washington's crippling of Tarleton's right hand in the duel). Again, when Tarleton was speaking sarcastically in the presence of her sister: "I would be happy to see Colonel Washington," he said, sneeringly. She instantly replied, "If you had looked behind you, Colonel Tarleton, at the battle of Cowpens, you would have enjoyed that pleasure." (*Lossing,* II, p. 436).

For an admirable study of the horse furniture and equipment of the Continental. Light Dragoons see Harold L. *Peterson's* "The Book of The Continental Soldier", Chapter 10, 'To Keep Horse and Man Together', pp. 202-217. The illustrations by Clyde A. Risley are superb. The saddles, bridles, holsters (for pistols), carbine buckets, valises and saddle bags and spurs are graphically portrayed by this excellent artist.

Of particular interest is Risley's plate on page 205 of the Third Continental Light Dragoons and how they looked in the south with the modified fringed Hunting Jacket. Note the iron protection bands on the Dragoon caps, which conform with F. P. Todd's fine plate in *Loescher,* page. 3.

The artist, Charles Willson Peale, a man of rare discernment in evaluations other than art, accompanied the 3rd Dragoons for a few days while they were en-route to South Carolina. Peale's Journal, penned at Wilmington, comments on the different degree of profanity in the northern and southern states. He notes that it was more pronounced amongst the 3rd Dragoons (a southern regiment) officers and men than northern inhabitants. Peale attributes it to the fact that southerners were "slave owners". (*Sellers,* 353-360). *******

PART FOUR
THE FOURTH CONTINENTAL LIGHT DRAGOONS

Principal Sources were:

CORRESPONDENCE of Colonel Stephen Moylan, in Pa. Mag., Vol. 37, July, 1913, pp. 341-360.

FITZPATRICK, John D., ed.,: Calendar of the Correspondence of George Washington . . . with the Officers, 4 Vols., Washington, 1915.

FITZPATRICK, John C.: Spirit of the Revolution, page 126.

GRIFFIN, Martin I. J.: Stephen Moylan, Philadelphia, 1909.

HEITMAN, Francis B.: Historical Register of the . . . Continental Army, Washington, 1914.

IMRIE, William: Series 71-74, Plate 28, U.S.A. (Colonial) 4th Continental Dragoons (Moylan's), 1779 by Carl Risley.

LEFFERTS, Charles M.: Uniforms of the American, British, French and German Armies . . . 1775-83, N.Y. Historical Soc., 1926. See Plate III, Moylan's Light Dragoons, 1779.

McCALL, Hugh: History of Georgia, Atlanta, 1909.

McCRADY, Edward: History of South Carolina in the Revolution, 1775-1780, N.Y., 1901.

MONAGHAN, F.: Stephen Moylan in the American Revolution, in Studies, September, 1930.

PENNSYLVANIA PACKET: April 3, 1779.

RESOLVES OF CONTINENTAL CONGRESS.

SIMCOE, John G.: Military Journal, New York, 1844.

TUCKER, Glenn: Mad Anthony Wayne & the New Nation, Chap. XVII, pp. 209-17, & Chap. XIII, 'Mad Anthony Recovers Ga.', Stackpole Books, 1973.

WASHINGTON, George: The Writings of George Washington, 39 Volumes, Washington, 1931-1944.

WOODHULL, Anna M. W.: Memoir of Brigadier General Anthony Walton White . . . , 1882, 11 pp. Presented to the N.J. Historical Society at Newark, May 18, 1882.

Some idea of the de-valuation of the Continental dollar relative to the purchasing of re-mounts for Dragoon regiments:

By 1780 the Virginia Assembly enacted into law limiting the price of cavalry horses at $150,000 *each,* or $150 sterling. Even that would only buy a very inferior mount.

An important factor overlooked by previous historians was the ability of the British army to buy their re-mounts with British Sterling, which was readily acceptable. This placed the American Continental Dragoon officers at a decided disadvantage with their *lowly* Continental dollar to barter with. This fact alone placed the British and Loyalist Cavalryman first in the field with much superior mounts.

The war took a drastic toll of American horses. The horse breeders and also the farmers were constantly harassed by American Patriots, Loyalists as well as British cavalrymen and their reluctance to give up their horses is understandable, the price notwithstanding. Consequently horse-breeding had come to a standstill by the end of the Revolutionary War and the new republic found itself starved for horses of all breeds and types, and many stallions and brood mares had to be shipped over from England.

The *Griffin* volume contains all of the important Revolutionary War papers of Colonel Moylan while commanding his 4th Dragoons. His many difficulties in recruiting and outfitting his regiment are in detail. Moylan wrote ninety four letters to Washington. A most valuable but little known documentary source, due to the rareness of the privately printed book.

The competition amongst the four Dragoon Regiments for crucial cavalry necessities was intense. Though Boston was the largest and most obvious center of supply in January 1778 (it being the largest "free city" to the Americans in the north) and fixed for the Second (New England) Dragoons, still, the geographical zoning was relaxed enough to allow Captain David Hopkins of Moylan's 4th to "penetrate" Boston for cavalry supplies. Actually, the supply sector designated for the 4th Dragoons was between the "North River and Susquehannah". However the two major ports of that area were New York and Philadelphia (the 4th's city of origin) then occupied by British. Both cities ironically were redundant with skilled craftsmen who were shut off to the 4th procurement officers.

Fitzpatrick's Calendar of the Correspondence of George Washington with his officers is invaluable, as well as the thirty nine volumes of *The Writings of George Washington.* These, and *Griffin,* are the prime source for the history of the 4th Continental Light Dragoons. A laborious compilation, or *Dragoon officer calendar* was constructed by this Author before beginning the writing of this book.

Regimental Standards

FLAG OF
SECOND REGIMENT LIGHT DRAGOONS
(PINK FIELD)

FLAG OF
SECOND REGIMENT LIGHT DRAGOONS
(BLUE FIELD)

Regimental Standards
of the
Continental Light Dragoon Regiments:

THE FIRST CONTINENTAL LIGHT DRAGOONS

Bland, with characteristic esprit de corps asked Washington for six camp colors and six standards, one for each troop (JRN CC, Dec. 11, 1976). There is evidence that the eventual Regimental Standard was a horse head with the words *First United States Light Dragoons.* This writer has never seen the flag but it is reported on exhibition in Bannerman's Military Museum, 501 Broadway, NYC.

The "horse head" on the standard would conform with Colonel Bland's April 13, 1977 "Uniform Order" stating ". . . the figure of a Horse and No. 1 Cast in the Button . . .", of the uniform coat.

Captain "Light Horse Henry Lee's" 5th troop of the First Dragoons having preceded Colonel Bland to General Washington and the New Jersey front, was rewarded by Bland when he arrived in December 1776 with the bulk of his Regiment. For Lee's valorous service, Bland in a brief but formal ceremony redesignated Lee's fifth troop as the first troop and given a small blue pennant or troop "Guidon" emblazened with white stars.- (*Gerson,* page 36).

THE SECOND CONTINENTAL LIGHT DRAGOONS

There were two Standards, one for Colonel Sheldon's first Squadron and one for Major Tallmadge's second Squadron.

Sheldon's Squadron Standard had a blue field with gold emblazenments for alternate (with blue) gold stripes in upper left corner for the thirteen states. On gold scroll in center of field the motto inscribed in Latin "PATA CONCITA FULMNT NATI" (The Country calls and her sons respond in thunder tones). On above gold scroll, also inscribed in black "2d Regt Lt Dragoons".

Tarleton claims to have taken one of the Standards (apparently there were three standards as both Sheldon's Tallmadge's Standards are accounted for later) in the Poundridge action on 2 July 1779.

Sheldon's blue Standard is (was?) owned in 1943 by Morgan B. Brainard, of Hartford, Connecticut, and for many years was deposited on loan with the Connecticut State Library on display to the public.

Tallmadge's Squadron Standard, as wide, but somewhat shorter in length than Sheldon's, was originally (reported) red. The field is now faded to an even pink, with silver, and pink strip in the canton, silver scroll shaded in green, edged in black with black lettering; silver wings, blue ball with buff clouds, and gold rays and thunderbolts (the same design as Sheldon's). The top scroll with the "2d Regt Lt Dragoons" is omitted on Tallmadge's Standard. The bottom scroll and motto inscription the same except for the "NT" omitted from the word "fulmnt".

Tallmadge's Standard was owned by Mr. Brainard's uncle, Senator Morgan G. Bulkeley, but mysteriously disappeared and its whereabouts was not known (in 1948), but apparently it has shown up in the Smithsonian Institute, Washington, D.C.

Both Standards of the Second Dragoons may be seen in color in *Schermerhorn, Frank Earle:* American and French Flags of The Revolution, 1775-1783, Pa. Soc. of Sons of The Rev., Philadelphia, 1948, Color Plate 6; *Peterson, Harold L.:* The Book of The Continental Soldier, page 160, Stackpole Books, 1968, Pa.

THE THIRD CONTINENTAL LIGHT DRAGOONS

The regimental Standard was conceived under romantic auspices. While courting Miss Jane Elliott, daughter of Colonel Charles Elliott, owner of "Sandy Hill" plantations near Charleston, after his regiment arrived in the south in 1780, the question of a Standard for his regiment arose and she enthusiastically agreed to fashion one for Colonel Washington, her financee.

She cut a square of crimson silk from the end of a rich damask curtain and made a flag with a fringed border, both border and field being red with a wreath of leaves with a curious inspection of: The 3 "horseshores" probably signifying "3rd Dragoons".

Mounted on a hickory pole the Standard was carried in all of the Third Dragoons battles from Cowpens to their last brave but futile charge at Eutaw Springs where the flag earned the title of "The Eutaw Flag". To commemorate their gallant charges there and the capture of their Colonel Washington.

The Flag may be seen in color in *Schermerhorn* and *Peterson*.

Colonel Washington's widow, the same Jane Elliott, in 1927 committed the flag to the care of the Washington Light Infantry, S.C. started in 1807 and still existant. To them the flag is almost sacred. —(*Schermerhorn,* page 81).

THE FOURTH CONTINENTAL LIGHT DRAGOONS

The Regiment undoubtedly had a Standard but as yet it has not turned up, or even a fragmentary description of it.

I would hazard a guess that the field may have been green with red in the inscription. Colonel Stephen Moylan was an Irish Catholic. There may have been a religious invocation in the motto.

·Dale Crawford '77·

Dale Crawford 77.

Plate 1, page 176
BLAND'S VIRGINIA HORSE
THE FIRST REGIMENT OF CONTINENTAL DRAGOONS

Plate 2, page 177
SHELDON'S CONNECTICUT HORSE
THE SECOND REGIMENT OF CONTINENTAL DRAGOONS